THE NEW
XENOPHOBIA

TABISH
KHAIR

THE NEW
XENOPHOBIA

OXFORD
UNIVERSITY PRESS

OXFORD
UNIVERSITY PRESS

Oxford University Press is a department of the University of Oxford.
It furthers the University's objective of excellence in research, scholarship,
and education by publishing worldwide. Oxford is a registered trademark of
Oxford University Press in the UK and in certain other countries

Published in India by
Oxford University Press
YMCA Library Building, 1 Jai Singh Road, New Delhi 110001, India

ISBN-13: 978-0-19-946358-9
ISBN-10: 0-19-946358-1

Typeset in Trump Mediaeval LT Std 10/15
by The Graphics Solution, New Delhi 110092
Printed in India by Rakmo Press, New Delhi 110 020

I wrote this book in the hope (utopian as it is) that when my children, Adian, Safia, and Alice, grow into adulthood, they will have no cause to read it.

CONTENTS

ACKNOWLEDGEMENTS

Acknowledgements are due to Sébastien Doubinsky and Isabelle Petiot for encouragement and criticism, and to Jessica Woollard, Sharmila Sen, Malini Sood, Rupa Bajwa, Sten Pultz Moslund, and the editors and anonymous readers of Oxford University Press for editorial feedback and/or endorsement. This study was written between 2010 and early 2013, but illness and death in my family prevented its preparation for publication until 2015.

INTRODUCTION | STRANGE FEAR

In its annual report for 2005, the European Commission against Racism and Intolerance (ECRI)—the official European xenophobia watchdog—identified cultural racism as 'increasingly worrying' and noted that '[t]oday, the idea of "culture" appears to increasingly replace the idea of "race"'. This observation by ECRI helps us understand why some commentators talk of the 'spurious' difference between a Western 'civic' xenophobia and an Eastern 'ethnic' xenophobia.[1] Xenophobia is, obviously, not just a Western phobia, and yet, in recent years, there has been a feeling that it operates in different ways in the West and in the East. This feeling is a simplification, though it contains a grain of perception: it does appear that in affluent First World countries—mostly conceptualized in terms of the 'West' in ordinary talk—xenophobia is unlikely to take the shape of the sort of ethnic cleansing that one witnessed in former Yugoslavia, on the borders of this mythical 'West', or that one sees during Hindu–Muslim riots in India, or Sinhalese–Tamil tensions in Sri Lanka, or 'ethnic' conflicts in Rwanda, or the mutual purging of Shias and Sunnis in Iraq and Syria. That xenophobic violence does take place in the rich 'West' can be explained away as random explosions, such as that of occasional neo-Nazi gangsterism, or even given a 'legitimate' political face, most obviously in recent anti-Muslim protests in Germany. And yet, a number of scholars have also noted the different—seemingly non-ethnic, evidently civic—forms in which xenophobia thrives in sections of rich, First World countries too. Further, scholars have worried about the similarities and, more problematically, the differences (for instance, in matters like homophobia and anti-Semitism) in the stated objectives of the old ultra-right and some parties of the new ultra-right in Europe.

It has become relatively easy to spot some forms of xenophobia—the fire bomb in the letter box of an immigrant; the Jew, Muslim, or Hindu being chased down a street by skinheads; the persecution of religious minorities in Pakistan; the killing of people of a different 'ethnicity'; even the violent imposition of another language or an alien lifestyle on any people. These are what I bracket under 'old xenophobia'—forms of xenophobia that we have become aware of largely due to our knowledge of the eighteenth-, nineteenth-, and twentieth-century history, culminating in the holocaust. And yet, as the above statements imply, there seem to be newer forms of xenophobia that do not fit this old and familiar rubric. We are obviously in a phase of history when we need to not just reinterpret the mechanisms of older forms of xenophobia, but also create the theoretical and cognitive structure to identify new forms of xenophobia.

A cursory look at the computer screen informs us that 'xenophobia' comes from the Greek words ξένος (xenos), meaning 'stranger' or 'foreigner', and φόβος (phobos), meaning 'fear'. Hence, xenophobia is defined as 'a groundless or unreasonable fear of foreigners or strangers or of that which is strange'. As strangers are inescapable for human social animals and fear is a very basic emotion that has had many evolutionary uses, it is inevitable that different socio-historical contexts will or can give rise to different types of xenophobia: while 'strangers' and 'fear' remain human universals, so to say, who we consider to be a stranger and what we fear obviously alters with changes in human circumstances and thinking. Moreover, the fact that we need to fear a stranger can also not be taken for granted, either philosophically or socially. As such, it is obvious that xenophobia cannot be a mere combination of the 'stranger' with 'fear'; if it was so, we would not be able to function in the world. When the 'spurious alignment of emotion (fear) and object is pervasive, phobic behavior will ensue,' notes Damasio,[2] and this element is always forgotten when we defend a xenophobic act or statement by either correctly noting that some strangers (like drug-pushers, for instance) can be dangerous or by incorrectly establishing a natural link between fear and a particular object (the stranger).

In the context of this study, I see no need to distinguish between xenophobia and misoxenia, 'outright hostility towards and hatred of foreigners'. To some extent, xenophobia always has to be expressed, and thus contains an element of overt hostility. Xenophobia, because it partly distorts the conceptual matter of the other by bestowing on it the reductive 'face' of the feared/hated stranger or foreigner, always has a social form or enunciation. The construction and reception of the stranger of xenophobia, old or new, is always a matter of power, a relationship of power. It is in this sense that my study of xenophobia confines itself largely to the history of capitalism, as the dominant structure of power, which arises identifiably in the eighteenth century (though with older roots) and transforms itself, again identifiably, in the late twentieth century. One can define power as the ability of the self to act upon the existence and consciousness of others. The French philosopher Michel

Foucault wrote in his later works that power does not exist in either a concentrated or diffused form; power exists only when it is put into action.[3] The other, as Foucault's explanation goes, is essential as the subject of power. That is, power requires a subject. Foucault, like many other post-structuralists, largely dissociated power from physical structures of subjugation. I use the term a bit differently.

Power refers to any imposition, physical or not, of one consciousness upon another. There seems to be no reason to disassociate the physical structures of power from its non-physical structures, as both exist only in relationship to one another. My quarrel is not with power, but with some of its usages and inequalities. I agree with Foucault's claim that power need not involve violence. But I also do not delimit violence to only physical violence; instead, I think of it as Emmanuel Levinas, another French philosopher, conceived of it: 'Violence is to be found in any action in which one acts as if one were alone to act [...]. Violence is consequently also any action which we endure without at every point collaborating in it.'[4]

With the expansion of consciousness, also as expressed in social organization, power inevitably gets more abstract. The physical and material aspect never disappears totally, as all known consciousness is physically and materially embedded or constituted. However, it is also evident that in a complexly conscious society—with a variety of needs, wants, and skills, which inevitably translate into extensive production and corresponding exchange or trade—the physical and material enactments of power will be mediated and justified in increasingly abstract ways. The role of money—as medium and social relation—is crucial in this historical context.

As crucial is the fact that money aspires towards absolute abstraction as capital. I examine this in detail later in the book, but here it might be understood, temporarily, as expressed in the evaporation of money, qua cash and currency, and its steady transformation into nothing but numbers. It is not the transformation into numbers that is the problem; this transformation is more of a symptom. This cumulative process remains embedded in material locations and in physical definitions of power, despite increasing abstraction, as long as money retains its character as medium and social relation. The notion of money as medium and social relation necessitates a conception of in-groups and out-groups in material terms. But as money becomes abstract capital in predominant terms— as in high capitalism—the source of fear and the shape of the stranger change. It is no longer the fear, however abstract, that an embodied sameness feels for an embodied difference. Instead, the self of high capitalism increasingly sees itself and its power in such abstract terms that it fails to register the inevitable violence of any exercise in (abstract) power. The stranger of high capitalism is the other who simply offers his brutish body as distasteful evidence of the abstract relations of power that enable high capitalist lifestyles and states. The strangers of xenophobia are not random. Their strangeness— and the violence brought to bear on it—serves to reinforce dominant avenues of empowerment.

In a world prior to money or in a world where extensive monetization had not almost eviscerated other structures of power, one could expect such violence to be mediated through material avenues—the bigger individual, the larger group, the better weapons of conquest and conscription, the stronger social organization, the greater labour capacity. With the rise of trade and money, and of early and classical capitalism, we find a gradual abstraction of the avenues of power, and consequently the justification and operation of xenophobia, most clearly reflected in our definitions of violence. With extreme abstraction of money under high capitalism, we encounter a greater abstraction of violence, and hence a different conception of the stranger of xenophobia. The identification of the strangers of this new xenophobia depends not, for instance, on an alternative or different physicality, but on their bid to evade or oppose the abstract power of high capitalism, encountered in different ways in European social democracies and in the top echelons of more combative and uneven capitalist societies, like those of the United States or India. The violence brought to bear on strangers—to exile them or to consume them— grows more abstract, while at the same time any other kind of material violence gets more easily identifiable, and hence monstrous. That obvious kind of violence is, often and sometimes correctly, seen as a version of old xenophobia. Old xenophobia is monstrous, spectacular, and quickly identifiable. New xenophobia, which must be seen within the context of high capitalism, is less visible, just as 'hard' cash becomes less visible when money transforms into numerical high capital.

The fact that the stranger of new xenophobia is a descendant of the stranger of old xenophobia should not blind us to the qualitative difference in how they are made and controlled. These strangers may have darker complexions and similar features. But they are constituted as strangers in different ways under the regimes of old and new xenophobia. The violence done to them differs as well. If old xenophobia seems to depend heavily on 'push-out' violence, based on the identification, marking, and excision of real or imagined difference, new xenophobia operates with varieties of 'push-in' violence. These often do not even come across to us as violence per se, conditioned as we are by older categories of xenophobia. At its simplest, the conceptual category of new xenophobia is necessary to enable us to cope with the new structures of high capitalism under which strangers are created and limited. These differ from the structures of early, colonial, and classical capitalism in many ways, even though they are also connected in some ways.

At the core of this book is the fact, often elided by scholars, that even by a liberal definition, we live in a world structured unevenly by a theory of capitalism that is at odds with the actual practice of it. Capitalism was understood initially as a system of power building upon, in theory, the free circulation of labour, goods, and money/capital; but, in effect, it moves towards the emaciation of labour, goods, and even money by (abstract and numerical) capital. In other words, capitalism is supposed to be based on the free movement of capital, labour, and goods. But today labour is far less free to circulate than capital. This has partly been the case in the past too, but it has been grossly acerbated in recent decades with the rise of high or finance capitalism.

Despite talk of globalization, labour is clearly more chained than capital. More than that, capital is far more mobile—and seemingly 'real' than both money and goods, and increasingly independent of them. I argue in this book that old xenophobia was constituted by a capitalism based on production, labour, and goods. In contrast, new xenophobia is shaped by a capitalism that no longer has much connection to production, labour, or goods, as recent economic crises have repeatedly underlined.[5] This is the reason that new xenophobia is more evident in rich European welfare states. Unlike the United States and similar First World countries with exposed workers (where new xenophobia is still at times overshadowed by old xenophobia because of this exposed workforce), Europeans are faced with a contradiction they are not even willing to acknowledge at times. European prosperity depends on Europe's participation in a high capitalist world that enables their capital to flow across national borders. Yet, European welfare is based on strong controls imposed on the movement of (non-European) labour. The occlusion of the changing nature of high capitalism is essential to new xenophobia and its forms. In other words, as I will elaborate in the following chapters, Europe wants the benefits of capitalism, but is unwilling to pay the price.

Lest my singling out of Europe mislead us into thinking that the stranger of high capitalism has a national or even a continental place of residence, let me hasten to add that new xenophobia does not happen in sealed spaces, for the simple reason that high capital does not exist in sealed spaces—such as nation states—either. It does, however, happen more in certain spaces (First World ones with a heavily protected working citizenry, such as rich European welfare states), though it may also occur in other spaces in a more irregular manner (First World countries with largely exposed and unprotected workers, such as the United States; or Third World countries with a small immensely rich high-capitalist class, such as India). My focus per force will be on the former, but the latter spaces are also brought into discussion when necessary.

In the chapters that follow, I shall discuss in greater detail how the stranger of xenophobia has been constructed in recent centuries, with a special emphasis of the characteristics of high capitalism's stranger. I shall discuss the changing nature of xenophobia as we move from the spectacular violence of skinheads attacking immigrants, Jews being persecuted in Europe, communal riots and genocides, to the 'innocuous' violence of new xenophobia under high capitalism. This deceptive violence, as we shall see, may not be understood as violence at all by some; it is a kind of violence that may want to pull the stranger in, or consume them, instead of exiling them. Such violence might not mark the stranger out as different, but require that their difference be erased. I shall devote some space to capital, especially as it functions in this century because I see it as the most important structure for understanding the power relations that produce new xenophobia.

Modern languages, with good common sense, have completely different words for people who avoid strangers, words such as 'shy' or 'reclusive' in English. A xenophobe does not merely want to avoid strangers. A xenophobe is someone who wants to reduce or eliminate strangers. It is hard to imagine an acrophobe who goes about demolishing buildings and hills or an ambulophobe who cuts off his own legs! Such cases would be very rare, if they existed at all. But the case of xenophobes who roughen up or demean a particular kind of stranger is by no means rare anywhere in the world. The roughening up of strangers assumes a relationship of unequal power in material terms. What happens when power circulates in the form of abstract numbers? In what ways can a stranger be roughened up without physical violence? Once we start asking this question, we inevitably move from a discussion of old xenophobia to a discussion of new xenophobia.

We also move on to something rare in the efforts to understand and tackle xenophobia, which has been constructed and continues to be seen as a problem to do with people, whether addressed as groups or as individuals. Inevitably, the usual cures for xenophobia are focused on controlling people, either by providing them with better education and information so that they can overcome their so-called prejudices, or by controlling them from entering foreign lands as immigrants, refugees, etc. This book will argue that while, no doubt, people have a role to play, they are by no means the primary 'disease' to control in a bid to cure xenophobia, and even less so when it comes to new xenophobia.

1

THE MAKING OF A STRANGER

Any study of anti-colonial movements—ranging from slave revolts in the Caribbean to the Ghaddar of 1857 and the struggle for independence in India (in the first half of the twentieth century) to the Algerian war of independence—offers instances of resistance that carry clear xenophobic tones. For instance, when European women and children were killed as part of a rebellion or a struggle for freedom in all these parts of the world. But the same struggles also contain examples of resistance that are obviously more 'principled' and not aimed simply at a foreigner or stranger.

How does one understand such opposition and resistance? Can one call such people xenophobic, even when they are obviously reacting to an invasion? If one cannot, how can one simply dismiss the perception of, for example, Anders Behring Breivik, the Norwegian rightist-zealot who murdered about 76 people in twin attacks in Norway in July 2011 because, as his rambling 'manifesto' indicates, he feels that his country is being invaded by Muslims and immigrants? Is any act of resistance to a stranger naturally an aspect of xenophobia? If so, what happens to so many, perhaps all, kinds of 'just' group resistance, whether in terms of gender, class, or nationality? How can we distinguish between just resistance and xenophobic violence?

The fact that we have to ask questions like this today reveals a change in our thinking. There is a tendency in some circles to condemn any act of overt violence, which makes it impossible to talk of liberation or freedom or revolution in the ways in which these concepts were used less than a century ago. Some of it arises from a genuine objection: as Mahatma Gandhi put it'somewhere, an eye for an eye ends up making the whole world blind. Violence, it has been noted, spreads like a virus; it spreads by infecting others. Hence, it seems counterproductive to answer violence with violence.

And yet the fact remains: sometimes violence is done to people. Power is always being negotiated, bartered, and grabbed by individuals and groups, and this can happen with overt or covert violence. It can happen in ways that allow the other and/ or the out-group equivalent space to construct, empower, and unfold itself, or ways that deny and curtail that space, which is what happens with all kinds of xenophobia. People can be killed, countries invaded, economies crippled. Some violence, it can be argued, is in any case necessary; for instance, the policing violence of democratic states, which protects ordinary citizens from criminals like drug-pushers (some of whom, but not necessarily the majority, can be 'strangers'). Evidently, it is one thing to say that violence should not be propagated or preached as a remedy; it is another thing to maintain that it invalidates its objects. This is because violence, in many forms, exists and affects us even when no *physical* or *overt* violence takes place or seems to take place.

Before moving on to an examination of abstract and covert forms of violence later in this study, we need to look at some forms of physical violence associated with obvious examples of xenophobia, all of which have thousands of factual equivalents. A quintessential version is fictionalized in Chinua Achebe's

Things Fall Apart. Okonkwo, the flawed hero, is told that an entire neighbouring tribe (the Abame) has been wiped out by Europeans because the tribe had killed a strange European who had turned up on a horse from nowhere. Here, if we bracket the aspect of colonial retributive justice, we have a clear case of xenophobia: the European is killed for being a stranger (out of place). History gives us thousands of similar examples—the European missionary killed in the colonies; the Australian aborigine killed for trespassing on settler lands; the unarmed African-American shot by a white man because he looked suspicious, most recently in the controversial Trayvon Martin–George Zimmerman case.

In Achebe's fictionalized rendition, while the tribe has reasons to fear strangers who look like the (murdered) European, having heard tales of attacks and persecution by European colonizers elsewhere, this does *not* justify their action, as they had no way of knowing whether this particular European stranger was hostile or not, as at least one of Okonkwo's companions realizes: 'Never kill a man who says nothing. Those men of Abame were fools. What did they know about the man?'[1]

In some ways, this kind of stranger goes back to our most basic, and entirely deceptive, notion of strangers. This is the stranger as *someone from without*, as *someone totally unknown*. There are two basic problems with this definition. First, it is almost impossible for a *total* stranger to appear. When the stranger seems to appear from nowhere, he has already been constituted within 'us'. Even Columbus did not meet 'total strangers' in the New World—his strangers had already been constituted in the minds of his generations, through discourses as divergent as those of the noble savage, cannibalism, and, in the case of the English, prejudices relating to those 'niggers of

Europe' (as a living Irish novelist puts it), the Irish. This is why, despite not knowing their languages, Columbus and his men could so readily divide these new peoples into just two tribes, the Arawak and the Caribe, each with thoroughly known propensities.

I will illustrate this further a bit later in this chapter with the use of a *purely* fictional stranger, the literary vampire, who despite *not* existing in real life still contains not just what is unknown, but also what is thoroughly known. In short, there is no pure or total stranger in any society, also because (and this is the second problem with our myth of the pure alien) such a stranger would simply not be comprehensible. The vampire is an apt generic 'stranger' to use to illustrate this, as it is not just a fiction based on facts, but also a fiction rooted in the essential facts of capitalism, as Karl Marx intuited when he repeatedly described capital as a vampire, an invisible, fluid, dead power that lives off the blood of the living, coming alive to the extent that it renders the living dead. There is, of course, a prior history of this fiction of the vampire, and that too, as we shall see, grows out a very factual history of the struggle for power and dominance. The fictional vampire exists, paradoxically, as an index of and limit to factual 'normality'. This is not surprising. The strangeness of the stranger is always a definition of our own normality; without it the stranger ceases to come into being qua stranger.

It is, therefore, not surprising to come across incidents of xenophobic violence between many peoples who have lived together in the past (as the break-up of Yugoslavia reminded us recently, and as we are constantly reminded by the Sri Lankan strife, as well as by recently escalating conflicts in places like Libya or Iraq) and often still live together in the present with a degree of tolerance. A common such flashpoint in relations between people who mostly live and work together takes place when we have what are called Hindu–Muslim riots in India.

The most concentrated occurrence of such riots took place in the 1947–8 years of India's Independence and its aftermath when the country was partitioned (partly because of colonial manipulation and partly due to nationalist demands on both sides) into a Hindu-majority India and a Muslim-majority Pakistan. Studies of the Partition as well as of later Hindu–Muslim conflicts inevitably illustrate how people who have shared a culture, a past, or even a childhood, found themselves pushed into the position of *strangers* who had to be combated.

Evidently, in such instances, we have the traces of a stranger being constructed before our very eyes out of a familiar person; a certain understanding of self and other turns a person into not just a stranger, but a hostile or detestable one, a stranger who has to be eliminated. This stranger, who is just as common to xenophobia as the previous ('unknown') type, is also just as obviously *constructed*. While in both cases, the myth of the hidden danger represented by the stranger is raised as a justification, the fact remains that we are not talking of pure strangers. We are talking of strangers whose difference we know, and of differences that are visible to us. If these differences are hidden, this has been (argue xenophobes) done with an evil intention in order to keep them from becoming visible to us, so that we can be harmed unaware.

In both these common constructions of strangers (the 'pure stranger' and the 'stranger within'), we see the ways in which fear (also as detestation, hatred, etc.) overlaps with difference and with what can be called contact/border. Xenophobia, old or new, is constructed out of a selective amalgamation and formulation of these three elements: fear, difference, and contact/border.

Fear

As Nussbaum notes, fear is a basic and very primitive emotion.

Unlike compassion, which requires perspectival thinking and is thus available only to a few species of animal, and even unlike anger, which requires causal thinking about who is to blame for causing a harm, fear really does not require very elaborate mental apparatus. All it requires is some rudimentary orientation toward survival and well-being....[2]

Nussbaum states that the ability to be aroused by what threatens us—or is imagined to be threatening us—is at the core of fear, and hence it was and is a useful evolutionary trait. 'Without fear, we'd all be dead.'[3] But, she goes on to argue, that while fear can be valuable, its perception of the world is narcissistic, 'extremely narrow', and highly liable to distortions of both self-understanding and fantasizing about others.[4]

Hence, while recognition of the evolutionary role of fear is necessary, it is not at all sufficient in a bid to understand xenophobia. For one, as studies indicate, the level of xenophobia in many nations does not necessarily correspond with the intensity with which the stranger is feared within that nation.[5] This is not surprising as we are not really talking of evolutionary fear in the case of xenophobia; we are talking of a discourse that constructs a particular stranger (or out-group) as an object to be feared. Moreover, there is evidently a difference between fearing a stranger you encounter, unexpectedly, in your sitting room, and fearing a stranger you encounter in passing on the road outside (or the abstract stranger of a certain type), even if there is a misleading cognitive link (stereotyping and inductive errors, in Rydgren's terms)[6] between the two in terms of fear.

Unfortunately, this difference is obscured by many thinkers who, like the German essayist and poet Hans Magnus Enzensberger, state, that '[s]elf-interest and xenophobia are anthropological constants; they are older than all known societies'.[7] There are various problems here. For instance, one could as easily claim, from another perspective and with as much historical evidence, that altruism and xenophilia are anthropological constants; they are older than all known societies. For societies to come into being, obviously, individuals have to 'overcome' their fear of other individuals and their investment in pure self-interest and narcissism at least to a degree. One can trace this by foregrounding self-interest and xenophobia, as seen in many liberal bourgeois discourses, and as reflected in Enzensberger's comment, or one can, with as much justification, make cooperation, altruism, and even xenophilia the primary factors. One can start with one set or the other as *primary* factors—and with as much evidence.

It is more fruitful to see self-interest and altruism, xenophobia, and xenophilia as, all other factors being equal, tendencies of equal import in human beings as a collectivity, whatever these impulses might or might not be in specific individual human beings. There is no reason or evidence to privilege one set over the other as primary factors. What is sometimes presented as 'evidence' of a natural fear of strangers is dubiously constructed bio-determinism, not that different from now defunct bio-determinist theories regarding the shape of the skull or the moral and intellectual propensities of skin colour in the nineteenth century. They can be exploded by contextualizing the matter. For example, xenophobia is not a corollary of the proof (if it exists) that a cat and a dog naturally fear each other, as here we are discussing two different species. One can take such arguments to pieces, though they often flourish in media and even, indirectly, academia. Damasio argues, with credible scientific evidence, that animals or birds (including humans) are not 'innately wired' for composite constructs of fear. A chick, for instance, does not fear an 'eagle' at birth; instead it is wired to fear specific images, sounds, etc., such as that of a wide-winged, swift-moving shadow. Hence, animals or birds do not suffer from 'bear-fear' or 'snake-fear'; instead, they are wired to fear large forms, growling noises, etc.[8] What this suggests, in the context of xenophobia, is the cognitive impossibility of fearing a stranger qua stranger, and it also explains why we give the stranger-to-be-feared certain animalistic attributes—hooked nose, large size, wily eyes, sharp teeth, etc.—which help us construct the stranger in the image of the forms that might actually evoke some sort of instinctive fear in us.

Xenophobia among human beings cannot be based on the proof (if it exists) that two flocks of apes are inevitably hostile to one another (if they are) as again we are talking of a very different context, framed by limits of perception, association, and competition that vary hugely from those of human beings. Xenophobia is not 'natural' even if it can be proved that babies are often afraid of strange things or people, because the very survival of babies also depends on their ability to understand, grasp, accept, and relate to the totally strange world they are born into, and the strange beings, ranging from their parents and nurses to day-care workers, etc., who rear them. The bid to base complex factors solely in biological and individual aspects is simplistic in general: 'Culture and civilization could not have arisen from single individuals and thus cannot be reduced to biological mechanisms and, even less, can they be reduced to a subset of genetic specifications.'[9]

Though the 'biological' is explicitly or implicitly posited as a justification for xenophobic discourses of 'purity' (from caste and race to nationality and 'culture'), the fact remains that biology does not posit any kind of 'purity'—even in the evolutionary sense, we know that the mitochondria in all eukaryotic (including human) cells is a basically foreign body, that human bodies contain far more foreign cells than human ones, and that genetic transfer also takes place laterally across species.[10] The list is long—and almost totally ignored by ideologues employing a stubbornly incorrect understanding of 'biology' to militate against the stranger in society.

Finally, the identification of xenophobia as 'natural' by people like Enzensberger is also based on the false assumption that our sympathies are confined to those we know. This, as Terry Eagleton notes, is not true; people can feel more strongly about remote events and personalities than about their own siblings.[11]

In short, the problem we are faced with is not that strangers have evoked fear in the past across most known societies (though all known societies also seem to have parables and fables about treating strangers well, as the Bible, among other texts, reveals). What is more at issue is the fact that the feared stranger needs to be defined first, and this definition has changed in significant ways across periods and cultures. The stranger who led to the spawning of the Greek term 'xenophobia' was by definition from outside the Greek city state; the German Jews, so hated by Nazis, were, on the other hand, mostly urban, even cosmopolitan individuals. Obviously, the stranger-to-be-hated alters with given changes in socio-historical context. Moreover, all through history and in every society, there is evidence of *some* strangers being treated well and *some* being treated badly; entire groups have been received with love or hatred. Evidently, fear as an evolutionary factor is not an explanation of xenophobia.

If fear is to be a helpful motivator in [... our complex socio, political, economic] world, then people will have to form a conception of their own safety and well-being, and that of their society, that is considerably more complicated than the narrow evolutionary focus on short-term bodily safety, and they will have to engage in sophisticated thinking about what threatens that well-being.[12]

This illustrates both the fallacy of equating xenophobia with evolutionary fear, and provides us with an understanding of xenophobia: it is after all a version of fear that has been culturally and often politically worked over in complicated, if not sophisticated, ways. Whether it is either correct or justified is of course another matter altogether.

However limited it might be to use evolutionary fear to explain xenophobia, it remains an element that can be (and is) put to great xenophobic effect. The stranger's body, once defined as out of place and a threat (a monster, a vampire, an impurity, a contagion), can be easily eradicated; actually, that is the only option left to anyone who wants to survive. (It is not incidental that the really gory acts of violence in Bram Stoker's *Dracula* are performed by the good guys out to eliminate the threat of the vampire.) This is one of the reasons why the physical being and appearance of the stranger is such a major concern of old xenophobia.

In philosophical terms, the face of the other has to be discernible to the self; given the potential resistance that one embodied consciousness offers another embodied consciousness by its very presence in a world of non-conscious objects, it is, as Emmanuel Levinas suggests, the face of the other that says, 'Thou shalt not kill'. Not really, xenophobia argues back: the stranger, once constructed in terms of the vampiric body, is an other whose face bares the fangs of a murderous intention, and hence the self is 'entitled' to a kind of self-protective desecration. No wonder Jonathan Harker can see only his own face, not Dracula's, in the mirror right at the start of Stoker's novel. Vampires are not reflected in mirrors, as the myth holds. Neither, one can argue, are strangers, as others central to the self's identity, in the mirror of xenophobia. What one sees is a construct of the self, reacting with fear to this shared, negotiated existence that the very appearance of the other demands.

This indicates the fallacy of taking the term xenophobia literally; it is not just fear of *any* stranger, it is fear of a *particular* kind of stranger. What is at issue is a struggle for power, perceived as inevitable or necessary because of the very *nature* of that particular stranger. The good guys in Stoker's *Dracula* have no choice but to persecute, kill, and desecrate the vampire—strangers they see as threatening, and all who are contaminated by them. It need hardly be said that in many ways, at least one of the good guys is a stranger to another from the team, and the main vampire expert, Van Helsing, is a total stranger to all except one of them, but these strangers are *not* perceived as threats. Once again, deep understandings of selfhood determine this equation, not least the extant cultural definitions of 'West' and 'Christianity' in the case of *Dracula*. In short, a certain construction of *difference* is essential to xenophobia and the fear it sets out to evoke.

Difference

Like fear, 'difference' is a non-answer. We are surrounded by difference. We do not really notice, let alone fear or detest, most of these differences. You might differ from your spouse or friend in any or all of these areas: brand of clothes, vegetarianism, vacations in Italy, regular exercise and jogging, political affiliation, professional qualification, gender, sexual preferences, colour, religion, nationality, etc. But these will not make you fear your friend or spouse. And yet, almost all of these differences can be constructed in such a way as to make you fear *the* stranger. Hence, it is not the difference of the stranger that is feared when we are xenophobic; it is a certain construction and understanding of difference (which might or might not exist).

Interestingly, in many versions of xenophobia, the stranger might be less different from you, but will still be feared or hated more. For instance, a white racist in Texas is more likely to fear or hate a Black man from the next neighbourhood—though they may share language, location, nationality, etc.—than he might, given his political propensities, a suitably Aryan-looking man from Denmark or Germany. Or a set of circumstances (some political or economic development, for instance) can strip away the mask from the familiar face in front of you and reveal the hidden stranger with his vampiric intention, which can only be thwarted with violence on your part.

Differences are always graded against similarities: one of the remarkable things about the literary (and filmic) vampire is that it is and isn't human; it has a body and does not have a body. This means that the vampire has to look (almost) 'human', but also has to share physical characteristics with 'animals' (fangs, nails, relish for blood, Count Dracula scaling a wall on all fours, a vampire turning into a bat, etc.). Moreover, the vampire has to have a seemingly human body that does not *really* exist. It is, in the latter sense, that vampires do not just transform into animals (or into mist in some cases), but that their reflections cannot be seen or that, once the stake is driven through their heart, they crumble into dust.

The physicality of the vampire is just as necessary to its existence as is the difference in its physical being. At one level, this combination helps us explain the construction of a repugnant difference by all kinds of xenophobia until recently. David McNally points out, quoting scholars like Bildhauer and Mills, Jones and Sprunger, that early modern monsters were partly a secularized version of mediaeval monsters, but both traditions—and the literary vampire of the nineteenth century has its roots in them—shared a striking feature: the monsters had a visibly physical presence. They were 'unsettling hybrids, strange combinations of body-parts from different species [...] or images of corporeal distortion, such as multiple heads and oversize limbs'.[13] This, as McNally notes, could have xenophobic uses at least by the time of the early Renaissance: 'Social-geographical foreigners might be pathologized and monsterized in these terms, as Africans and the Irish frequently were.'[14] As we shall see, with the rise of modernity and capitalism, social behaviour (and not corporeal elements) slowly became the prime index of monstrosity, and this focus on the physical is one of the ways in which old xenophobia differs from new xenophobia.

The stranger, like the vampire, has a body that is like 'our' body, but not really so. The stranger, like the vampire, might be innocuous in broad daylight, but is always a hidden, dark, potential threat. The stranger, like the vampire, appears to be like 'us', but only by deception. The stranger, like the vampire, appears alive, but isn't really so. The stranger, like the vampire, can be killed without any commandment, sacred or secular, being really broken, because in some ways s/he is already dead in xenophobic eyes. The difference that is constructed, registered, highlighted, and, finally, feared in a stranger is a central concern of any study of xenophobia. Without understanding this difference, we cannot even talk of any fear of the stranger.

Border/Contact

Sheer difference is not enough, as, among others, Yuval has shown in a paper about the 'shared myths, common language' of Jews and Christians in Europe during the Middle Age.[15] There has to be a *meeting line* of difference; this is what I conceptualize in terms of 'border/contact'. Border/contact is defined as much by discourses as by actual living spaces (both material and cultural). Let us pause for a moment and go back to vampires in Gothic and Gothicized fiction in order to understand this.

The figure of the literary vampire, as a threatening interloper, the embodiment of a monstrous difference to be feared, and a potentially imperial stranger, can be traced to a mediaeval history of folk beliefs and superstitions, but it also has to be understood in its eighteenth- and nineteenth-century manifestations within a nexus of what I shall term border/ contact.[16] This includes, in occluded forms at times, elements from before the eighteenth century. For instance, the aristocracy of the main vampire has at least something to do with European feudalism, when seen in the light of Perry Anderson's observation of the conflict of interests between peasants and feudal lords.[17] Here, we have some of the elements that went into the vampire narrative as retrieved from folk sources in the eighteenth century. In other words, the constitution of a different caste—in due course, 'aristocrats'—who preyed on the people from above, who were considered a breed apart, but who depended on the 'life-blood' of the common people. This is also, in *spatially* segregated class terms (on both sides), the monster embodied as a physical difference to be feared, an essential aspect of mediaeval accounts of the monstrous.[18]

But, as is the case with such symbolic retellings, eighteenth- and nineteenth-century narratives of the vampire (from Camilla to Dracula, aristocrats all) did not just contain memories of the past; they also contained glimmerings of the present. The vampire in this sense reflects, as scholars like Franco Moretti[19] and Ken Gelder have shown, the advent of early capitalism as well as the fact that, by the eighteenth century, aristocrats were seldom rooted in their country seats or family castles. They were more likely to visit such sources of their wealth— 'life-blood'—from other metropolitan spaces and, in the case of plantations in colonies, from home countries in Europe. Also, by the eighteenth century, in the light of Enlightenment discourses and the political radicalism of the American and French revolutions (with their championing of equality, liberty, fraternity), an aristocrat who lived off the fat/blood of the land was not only seen as a throwback to an earlier tyrannical state (and hence basically 'dead' and alive only as the 'undead'), but also as vicious, exploitative, devious, bestial: a vampire.

Folk impressions of feudalism as well as cultural and historical border/contact zones in the case of the middle-class writers and readers of vampire narratives in the eighteenth and nineteenth centuries partly explain the aristocratic nature of vampires in European narratives. But this was by no means the only set of border/contact factors, for the experience of difference was not situated simply on the aristocracy–bourgeoisie–peasantry axis. Various other experiences and conceptualizations of difference—an obvious one that I will leave out, but that again informs vampire narratives is that of the 'deviant' female—had already framed the worldview of Europeans by the eighteenth century. For instance, Judaeophobia (nourished by a certain reading of the Jew in the light of the Bible as well as early Christian suspicion of usury), the Islamic threat, prejudice against Gypsies (nourished, among other things, by the unsettled nature of Gypsy life over centuries of settled agriculture and urban commerce), etc., as they existed and evolved in eighteenth-century Europe. The vampire— as a grossly *different* stranger who could only be *feared* and eliminated—grew out of such spaces of *border/contact*.

Obscured Familiarity of Strangers

Like the vampire, the stranger of xenophobia is a source of fear because of a certain construction of difference, and this happens because of the existence of a space (often occluded or denied) of border/contact. No stranger is a pure stranger. This was brought home to me with particular force some years ago, when I was discussing recent migrant literature by Muslim authors based in Europe. It was an introductory class in a Danish university and, as far as I could see, the class contained only Scandinavian and German students. The discussion had veered, predictably, to the status of Muslims in Europe and most students were of the opinion that many of the problems related in the novels under review had to do with the fact that 'Muslims are new-comers to Europe'. Then a young woman, blonde, blue-eyed, and very Scandinavian-looking to me, raised her hand from the back row. She intervened with these words: 'I disagree that Muslims are new to Europe. I am a Bosnian Muslim and my family has been European, and Muslim, for centuries.'

If one excavates the silence that this young woman's statement made momentarily audible in my class, one gets an understanding of not just the vampire in European fiction, but also the greatly troubling Muslim stranger in contemporary Europe. We are talking of border/contact once again. Here I have in mind, in particular, the Enlightenment reconstitution of Europe in the light of a 'return' to Reason after the so-called Dark Ages, which, following the earliest decades of the Enlightenment, led to an endeavour whose consequences are with us today. These consequences covertly negate the universal claims of a rational Enlightenment, by cocooning Europe in itself. Any study of the Enlightenment that does not take this remapping of border/contact into account—and such studies were the rule rather than the exception until recently—in fashioning a critique of the limits of Enlightenment universalism is, by definition, deeply ideological.

Recent studies have noted the ideological limits of such an occlusion or evasion in two ways:

1. By highlighting that the 'classical' Greek and Roman civilizations to which Europe-purist versions of the Enlightenment allude were by no means purely European. The Mediterranean, as one author has put it, is basically a lake between Europe, Asia, and Africa, and Greek and Roman civilizations flourished all around it. Some of the greatest names associated with Greek and Roman cultures were born in Africa or Asia Minor. Various influences crisscrossed the Mediterranean, as did people. The early Greek thinkers, for instance, acknowledged cultural and intellectual loans from Egypt. In that sense, Christianity, when it finally came to Europe, was not something from unknown territories for the literate classes. Right from the genesis of Judaism, with the flight of Moses from Egypt to the birth of Jesus in Bethlehem, paid homage to by the three wise men from the East, classical Europe represented a culture marked by what would today be called African, Asian, and European elements and sources. (This was, of course, also true of much of 'classical' Africa and Asia.)

2. By highlighting the evasion or reduction of the Arabic (and Moorish) contribution to both the preservation and

development of this so-called 'European' classical heritage and the fact that at least early Enlightenment thinkers and scholars in Europe were fully aware of this reality. Jonathan Lyons's *The House of Wisdom* is a recent, concise, and readable account of this. Not only does it provide a description of the Arab contributions to the Enlightenment, but it also recovers stories of early Enlightenment scholars, such as the twelfth-century Abelard of Bath, who made a dedicated effort to learn from the Arabs. As Lyons puts it,

[t]he arrival of Arab science and philosophy, the legacy of the pioneering Abelard and those who hurried to follow his example, transmuted the backward West into a scientific and technological superpower [...]. The power of Arab learning, championed by Abelard of Bath, refashioned Europe's intellectual landscape. Its reach extended into the sixteenth century and beyond, shaping the ground-breaking work of Copernicus and Galileo. This brought Christian Europe face-to-face with the fact that the sun—not the earthly home of God's creature, man—stood at the centre of the universe. Averroes, the philosopher-judge from Muslim Spain, explained classical [Greek and Roman] philosophy to the West and first introduced it to rationalist thought. Avicenna's *Canon of Medicine* remained a standard European text into the 1600s. Arab books on optics, chemistry, and geography were equally long-lived.[20]

As Lyons and other recent scholars have noted,[21] early Enlightenment thinkers in Europe were largely aware and appreciative of this debt to Arab and Moorish learning. Even as late as the thirteenth century, Roger Bacon, probably the first proponent of the scientific method in England, could openly acknowledge that Europe owed its philosophy to 'the Muslims' while also accusing Muslims of becoming lost in 'sensual pleasures because of their polygamy'. This, as Lyons notes, marked the 'West's wilful forgetting of the Arab legacy ... [due to] anti-Muslim propaganda crafted in the shadow of the Crusades'.[22] The new 'Western' message regarding Islam, further reinforced during the Renaissance when the West looked for sustenance and support to an idealized and deracinated notion of Classical Greece, comprised

> four central themes, a number of which still resonate today: Islam distorts the word of God; it is spread solely by violence; it perverts human sexuality, either by encouraging the practice of polygamy, as in the famed harems of the sultans, or through repressive or excessively prudish attitudes; and its prophet, Muhammad, was a charlatan, a tool of the Devil, or even the Antichrist.[23]

Does it even need to be pointed out why the vampire faces the East, so to say, in eighteenth- and nineteenth-century European narratives? Even with Islam vanishing from the matrix, its 'horrors' remain—and are crucial to the identity of the vampire. However, like the vampire, the 'new' Muslim in Europe, is by no means a 'total stranger'.

To sum up, the construction of certain kinds of 'difference' across (un)faced border/contact zones is central to the creation of xenophobic fear. There is always the presence of this border/ contact zone, which is distorted or ignored in the construction of difference, and this combination is essential to the fear evoked by the stranger. In these terms, the stranger—once defined as someone who is foreign in the sense of not belonging (and this definition gets more complex and insidious with the greater complexity of societies, which expands the border/ contact zones in material as well as symbolic senses)—can also be understood in terms not dissimilar to those employed by Mary Douglas to discuss traditional and folk ideas of 'dirt':

If we can abstract pathogenicity and hygiene from our notions of dirt, we are left with the old definition of dirt as *matter out of place*[24] [...]. It implies two conditions: *a set of ordered relations and a contravention of that order* [...]. Dirt is the by-product of *a systematic ordering and classification of matter*, in so far as ordering involves rejecting inappropriate elements.[25] (Italics mine)

This 'ordering and classification of matter' was essential to the creation of the stranger, as a threat to be feared, by old xenophobia: it is this process that I have traced in this chapter as involving the evocation of fear (as a misleadingly natural response to the stranger) by constructing a particular kind of difference based partly or entirely on obscured and distorted zones of border/contact. Xenophobia, as we have experienced it until recently, always had to define the 'body' of the stranger, so that it could be negated because, as is the case with the vampire, this is a body of deception and difference; it is *matter out of place*.

2

THE CHANGING FACE OF XENOPHOBIA

There is a powerful anti-colonial myth that I heard being repeated by people in Bihar (among the first regions in India to be colonized by the British East India Company), when I was growing up there. It recalls the misery caused to weavers in northern and eastern India by the British East India Company. It is claimed that, in order to deprive them of their livelihood and market, the East India Company 'cut off' the hands of Indian weavers in the late eighteenth and early nineteenth centuries.

Like some other accusations of gory atrocities on both sides of the colonizer/colonized divide, this charge is not substantiated by historical evidence. Historians agree that officials or adherents of the East India Company did not go about chopping off the hands of Indian weavers. But historians also agree that the introduction of mass factory-produced and cheap textiles from the UK and the imposition of various tariffs and other controls on Indian weavers did deal them a debilitating blow, causing much suffering and starvation.

However, the myth of chopped hands is significant in the context of my general thesis in this book: the fact that, until the rise of capitalism, power was predominantly imposed, maintained, and experienced in physical and material terms.

Seemingly abstract institutions such as 'family' or religion (most powerfully expressed in the predominance of rituals, lifestyles, and religion-based hierarchies) had strong physical and material moorings. Even money, until it refined itself into abstract capital, could only be understood as a 'medium of exchange' and/or a 'social relation', both of which return us to the bodily networking of power and privilege. The opposition of Axial-age religions to money (especially in the form of interest) was based on a perception of the logic of capital embedded in monetary economies, but this logic was still not overwhelming enough as long as capital remained largely embedded in money *as* a medium of value/trade and a social relation.[1]

In common parlance (and in under-theorized economics), there is a trend these days to differentiate between 'good capital'—when people work for their money—and 'bad capital'—when money works for people, that is, when money is used to breed more 'money'. It has become increasingly evident that the latter is what many of the rich do, and more so in high capitalism. I do not accept this definition of capital, as if it was a Hollywood actor capable of playing both the good and the bad guys. It is much better—and clearer—to differentiate between money and capital. When people *work* (create, produce, service, construct, etc.), and when they are paid for it, what they earn is basically 'money'—it is a medium of exchange and a social relation. It is when this money is used to spawn more money— without any added value from the only source that can add value to money, which is human labour—then, and only then, are we talking of 'capital'. Capital, by definition, is not just a 'medium of exchange', and under conditions of advancing capitalism, it also ceases to be a 'social relation'. Its logic and existence become increasingly independent of both the goods produced/exchanged and of the buyers and sellers in a market, as is basically attested by both Marxists and Liberal capitalists, though in different words. We will return to this point later on, but here it enables us to explain the myth of the weavers of India and their 'chopped hands'; until capitalism, almost the only way to stop 'free' (not 'slave') weavers as a community from weaving was, in effect, to chop off their hands (or heads). As the value created by what they sold depended on their bodily skills, and as they could take those skills elsewhere along with their bodies in a world where various local and regional markets had not been fused into a universal capitalist market, the metaphor of 'chopping off their hands' worked very well to signify the consequences of the British capture of the textile market in India, via a combination of imperial power and capitalism.

The 'chopped hands' actually become a metaphor for the power of imperial/colonial capitalism to render weavers 'handless' by restricting their opportunities and flooding the universal market with cheap mass-produced textiles from elsewhere *without* any physical constraint being placed on them. The weavers of India did get their hands chopped off *symbolically*, for now it was no longer necessary to do so *literally*. However, an aspect of physical power—colonial conquest and regulations—was still necessary to achieve this. The metaphor of chopped-off hands takes into account both these aspects of early and colonial capitalism. It is the aspect of the greater abstraction of capital as power that I will examine in detail in the succeeding pages.

I have indicated, with the help of a purely fictitious kind of hated stranger, the vampire, that xenophobia works in a complex manner; by insisting on the physical/material difference of the stranger to be hated, it simultaneously negates the body of the stranger as otherwise entitled to the same kind of treatment as 'our' bodies. If the physical or material difference of the stranger-to-be-hated/feared is not visible, then this merely suggests a hidden difference, and hence *heightens* the diabolical nature of the stranger. This stress on a material and physical difference can be understood with reference to a pre-capitalist and early capitalist structure of power—power embedded in the body, or in a structure of goods produced and carried over for trade by the body, or monies exchanged (as medium and social relation) by the body.

What I have called old xenophobia is based on this conception of the strangeness of the stranger. But it is affected by other matters, particularly the rise of classical capitalism, with its increasingly abstract structures of power. Hence, for instance, from the body of the slave as a particularly controlled subject–object within a larger network of physical and material social relations, we move, in the eighteenth and nineteenth centuries, to the body of the slave not just as goods or wealth— which it could have been in the past too—but as ancillary and subservient to a global networking of abstract capital. I will trace something similar with reference to the rise of nationalism and the transformation of Europe's ancient culture of Judaeophobia to Nazi anti-Semitism.

But here, it is sufficient to stress that what we experienced as old xenophobia even in the first half of the twentieth century needs to be understood in this context: it was based on the assumption of a physical difference, explicit or hidden in the stranger to be feared/hated, which was, however, itself increasingly shaped by abstract and ideal factors introduced by capitalism. Nazism, in many ways, was a regressive reaction *also* because it took this logic of old xenophobia to an extreme— marking, segregating, and exterminating the stranger physically while also adducing moral, spiritual, and even intellectual grounds for the genocide of Jews, Gypsies, Slavs, etc.

We need to understand, but also go beyond this largely physical conception of xenophobia. With the rise of high capitalism, while power may still be negotiated along physical and material avenues, capital affords a highly abstract channel of empowerment that creates a different kind of stranger-fear/ hatred and its enactment. This has to be understood in separate terms too; new xenophobia (like old xenophobia, a term of convenience), might have a symbiotic relationship to old xenophobia, but it can also use aversions to old xenophobia to justify and implement its own 'new' hatreds and inequalities. The strangeness of the stranger is perforce defined differently in a different networking of power.

It has become easy for us to spot the forms of old xenophobia. While there are still surprisingly many who remain stubbornly racist and anti-Semitic in nineteenth-century ways, most thinking and educated people 'do not have problems with Jews or Blacks'. As a recent article in *The Guardian Weekly* puts it, 'No one's ever racist nowadays. But somehow racism still seems [...] to find its targets.'[2] Mostly people do not believe in segregation along racial lines. They definitely do not say out aloud that they want separate buses for Blacks or separate schools for immigrants. If they suggest it, and very few do so openly, they adduce semi-abstract explanations: a sociology of criminality, the power of culture, the superstitions of religion, the need for special language, and other training, etc. As Roemer, Lee, and van der Straeten put it, even conservative positions on the 'race issue' in the USA [and elsewhere] often use the 'code words of "law and order"'.[3]

Actually, in at least some circles, a counter-movement can be observed; any bid to discuss inequalities or contextual differences in terms of categories that can be given a physical or material dimension, ranging from race to class, is sometimes dismissed as prejudice. In the process, often, the very inequalities are dismissed too. The problem is partly a conceptual one. It can be best encapsulated in this statement: while our claims to rights have to be universal in order to be just, we are always oppressed only in our particularities. No one is oppressed as a 'human being'; we are oppressed as women, gays, immigrants, etc. On the other hand, any claim to rights that is not extended to the human being becomes, by definition, an exercise in power and prejudice, and not a universal claim to rights.

In the light of our discussion of old xenophobia, though, what is remarkable about forms of new xenophobia is their tendency to erase or overlook the physical particularities of the stranger. Old xenophobia was faced with the problem that not all strangers looked physically different; this was also because 'friends' could and did become 'strangers', in changed power contestations of border/contact, as in many nationalist uprisings and reactions. This problem was counteracted by positing a diabolical hidden difference and, for that reason again, it led to a pronounced marking and segregation of the stranger, as the Nazis did with Jews. Because the stranger, though secretly different, was trying to pass as one of us, s/he had to be tagged and isolated under old xenophobia.

Zygmunt Bauman's discussion of the two common strategies employed by societies usually to deal with strangers or difference—'*anthropophagic*: annihilating the strangers by *devouring* them [... and] *anthropoemic*: vomiting the strangers, banishing them from the limits of the orderly world and barring all communications with those inside'[4] (italics in original)—is pertinent in this context. To add to Bauman, there was a kind of anthropophagic strategy, at least in pre-modern societies, which provided somewhat greater respite to strangeness of a certain sort, for instance (also as discussed by Foucault) the conflation of madness with inspiration or divinity. In her illuminating book, Julia Kristeva suggests that the patterns of assimilating the 'different human being' into 'the fraternities of the "wise", the "just", or the "native" [in] Stoicism, Judaism, Christianity, and even the humanism of the Enlightenment' marked a 'genuine rampart against xenophobia'.[5] This is not the way I see such, and other (such as Islamic or Hindu), bids to assimilate the foreigner or stranger; any assimilation that depends on the re-naming of the foreignness or strangeness of the 'different human being' cannot be considered a sufficient rampart against xenophobia (though it can be a provisional one), despite the fact that it is better than the obviously xenophobic option of hounding the foreigner to death.

It can be argued that old xenophobia stressed the anthropoemic aspect, and new xenophobia stresses the anthropophagic aspect, if one employs Bauman's terms. This would be partly true, but also deceptive. This is so because, traditionally, the anthropophagic strategies ended in the total consumption of the stranger; the stranger merged with us and became one of us. New xenophobia does *not* posit this total merger, as we shall see. The stranger, under new xenophobia, remains a stranger, but is not allowed to *exhibit* signs of his/her difference. The strangeness of the stranger is not located physically or bodily, but moved to a sphere of abstraction, which is in some ways similar to 'value' in the abstract nature of capital in high capitalism.

One way of understanding this would be to look at the most common irruptions of Islamophobia in Europe today, which—being 'developed' and hence high capitalist to a large extent—offers some early examples of the trend. This Islamophobia shares some elements with older Judaeophobia and anti-Semitism, as has been pointed out by various scholars, but it differs in one major way. The similarities are more obvious. They include the common linking of Jews and Muslims with deception, the anti-Christ, and the Devil, certain physical characteristics, rabid sexuality and lechery, ritualistic orthodoxy, secretive societies, etc. It is today often forgotten that, just as Muslims are nowadays portrayed as a circumcised people who pray all the time and whose men seduce and control women, Jews were also condemned for exactly these characteristics well into the twentieth century.[6]

The difference is less obvious, and needs to be conceptualized with reference to the most emotive political issues regarding Muslims in Europe in recent years. As a rule, these revolve around the attempt, real or perceived, by Muslims to *make* their differences physically visible, whether it is through male and female clothing, or distinctive architecture, or just the fact of congregating for some purposes (namaz) and in some neighbourhoods. If Jews were segregated and tagged under old xenophobia, Muslims are put under pressure *not* to tag themselves or to segregate under new xenophobia. They are never really 'assimilated', in the sense of the anthropophagic strategies of old xenophobia, for the fact of their Muslimhood (often raised to an abstract level of idealist, cultural, and moral issues, such as the contention or belief that 'they are not capable of democracy') makes them perpetual strangers, but they are expected to keep this difference as invisible as possible. Throughout Europe, in France, Denmark, Switzerland, etc., the greatest and most emotive demonstrations against Muslims in the past decade or two have involved the attempt, usually by a very small number of Muslims, to make their difference visible, either by constructing a minaret (or because of the fear that they would construct a minaret), or by dressing in particular ways. In Denmark, it took the Muslim communities

decades of petitioning, etc., before they were finally allowed to
have a graveyard of their own, about a decade ago. The 2009
referendum, when almost 60 per cent of voters in Switzerland
voted against the construction of minarets, often with reference
to elaborate verbal and visual symbolism, was just one of many
such events in Europe. Another such instance was the campaign
poster of the far-Right Swiss People's Party, which presented
a flattened red–white flag of Switzerland foreshadowed by a
dark, veiled woman, and pierced by dark minarets shaped like
missiles.

While some of these protests have other well-springs too,
such as the feminist element in the protests against the veiling
of women, the fact remains that they have been applied to
stereotype and browbeat a complex and large group of peoples;
this assigns to them typically xenophobic tendencies. But they
differ glaringly from old xenophobia in this: if old xenophobia
would have encouraged the tagging and segregation of (real,
presumed, or constructed) physical difference, new xenophobia
protests against it.

Why is that so? I have two overlapping answers to this
question: the changing face of immigration under high capitalism and the changing face of the welfare state under high
capitalism.

Immigration, High Capitalism, and the Welfare State

The fall of the Berlin Wall, as all contemporary media accounts
illustrated, was meant to announce a brave new world. This
was, partly, a world beyond the forms of old xenophobia
witnessed in the early decades of the twentieth century and, to

some extent, embodied by the Berlin Wall for many in the 'free' West. Suddenly, we had a very physical/material demarcation between a recently created 'us' and 'them' being taken apart in a world that was supposed to have overcome most of the old forms of violence, exemplified in the history of repression and nationalism (built upon the older traces of racism and Nazism) that the wall had come to signify. Its fall was supposed to signify the end of that world of physical segregation and repression. The wall, after all, was very real, a material fact out there. Suddenly, with it being demolished brick by brick, we had a 'free' world, one without such physical barriers to freedom and an intermingling of peoples. This is no doubt one side of the story.

The other side is this one:

According to a 2006 study carried out by the Berlin Wall Association and the Centre of Contemporary Historical Research, 125 people were killed trying to cross the Berlin Wall throughout its entire history. Between 1988 and April 2011, 15,551 immigrants died trying to cross Europe's borders, according to the anti-racist organization, United.[7]

The majority of these deaths occurred far from any concrete 'wall'; they took place on open stretches of sea, being traversed by unseaworthy vessels full of desperate immigrants, and sometimes not aided by First World vessels or actually turned away from land; they took place in no-man's land, and in forests and various other kinds of less visible borders. And we are not even counting deaths from starvation, malnutrition, and such less obviously physical types of violence in refugee camps, etc. Immigrants, as Carr points out, have not just died trying to reach the West, but they have also killed themselves within the borders of the West. In Germany alone, between 1998 and 2000, '150 people killed themselves [...] because they were due to be deported'.[8]

Obviously, there are walls and there are 'walls', just as there is violence and there is 'violence'. A failure to conceptualize this is a failure to face up to the changing face of xenophobia. To understand the changes that have taken place, we need to consider the following three factors:

1. Changing patterns of immigration in and from the mid-twentieth century.
2. Changes in capitalism, or, in other words, the movement from production-based capitalism to high capitalism, finance capitalism, or 'globalization'.
3. Changes in the socio-political organization in the First World, particularly Europe, with the rise and crisis of social welfare states.

Changing Patterns of Immigration

Between 1800 and 1930 alone, '40 million Europeans migrated permanently overseas, mainly to North and South America and Australia',[9] which (if one factors in the lower European and world populations) would come to many times that number in comparative figures today. This number does not include the millions who went abroad, largely on empowered terms as colonizers or backed by colonial power, to make a fortune elsewhere, and then returned to Europe. But the decades of decolonization after World War II marked a significant change:

For much of the nineteenth and early twentieth centuries, the great migratory movements that shaped European history were directed outwards to the Americas and the colonial world, or took place within the continent itself. In the years that followed World War II, this historic pattern was reversed, as a number of European countries tolerated or actively encouraged immigration from the Third World and their former colonies in order to make up for the post-war shortage in unskilled labour.[10]

This new migratory phenomenon ran into the prejudices of old xenophobia that existed within European borders, but— given post-war economic needs—was 'tolerated' and used. However, with the economic and political climate changing, this compromise started cracking after just two decades, though the pieces took longer to crumble; by the 1980s, legal avenues of migration for unskilled or semi-skilled Third World labour had mostly dried up in Europe.[11]

Hence, what we are talking of—and I will save space by not adducing common data and examples—is a *perceived* rise of immigration to developed countries in the middle decades of the twentieth century, and a slowing down (in relation to world population) from the 1980s onwards. This is a valid perception, but also misleading if one does not put it in a larger economic and cultural context. Figures on population and migration are full of ambivalent factors, such as the difference between foreigners and citizens of foreign origin, which is often occluded in xenophobic and even in most nationalist accounts, and the fact that most foreigners live in countries near their home nations. Hence, for instance, there are far more Germans in Denmark than Nigerians or Indians, just as there are far more Bangladeshis and Tibetans in India than in Denmark. The many Germans in Denmark are seldom what Danish xenophobes notice, and while they do notice the few Bangladeshis and Tibetans, they fail to recall that actually most Bangladeshi and Tibetan immigrants/refugees are to be found in India!

In other words, to use such figures with any degree of scientific contextualization and accuracy calls for a closer look at changes in capitalism over largely the same period. This is lacking in the case of xenophobes; it is rare even in the case of many media commentators and some scholars. I will spend some time and space on it in the next subsection.

Changes in Capitalism

It was not as if the earlier nation-based model of capitalism was not international; capitalism is based on trade, and has always been thoroughly global in its reach. It is this that Giddens meant when he described that period—the one I associate with early and classical capitalism (old xenophobia) as against high or 'global' capitalism (new xenophobia)—in these words: Capitalism is 'international in its scope' and also that 'a capitalist society is a "society" only because it is a nation state.'[12]

But the champions of globalization are not altogether wrong either; something unprecedented did happen in recent decades. Let us look at some hard facts first. Using quantitative data borrowed from the work of Francois Morin and a 'synthetic table' that, because it would be obtuse to non-economists, I have left out, the economist Samir Amin spells out a significant change in capitalism in recent decades:

Goods and services transactions (of world GDP) represented 3 per cent of the monetary and financial transactions conducted in 2002; transactions concerning international trade amounted to hardly 2 per cent of the foreign exchange transactions; settlements of purchase and sale of shares and bonds in organized markets (operations considered as being constituents by excellence to capital markets) amounted to only 3.4 per cent of all monetary settlements! It is transactions in hedging products—designed to cover the operator's risks—which have literally exploded! [...] *The ratio between hedging operations and production and international trading was 28:1 in 2002—a disproportion that has*

been constantly growing for about the last twenty years and which
has never been witnessed in the entire history of capitalism.[13] (Italics
mine)

One can also put this from another angle: for instance, with
reference to the so-called 'financialization thesis', which 'in
[the] USA implied a drastic increase in the sphere of corporate
profits of the financial sector in relation to the non-financial
corporate profits from 25.7 percent in 1973 to 49.7 percent in
2000'.[14] Or, in yet other words that mean the same thing, we
can note that $1.9 trillion changes hands (mostly as numbers)
every day on the global markets, and this is 50 times greater
than the total value of all goods and services traded globally
each year![15]

In simpler words, much of current capital does *not* exist
as goods, trade, or even cash *any longer*; it exists as a play of
numbers. What it produces is not goods, commodities, and
even services, but more numbers, mostly. Finance capital as
it circulates in the world today, largely from one metropolis to
another, does not produce value in terms of goods, production,
and trade; it simply reproduces itself and multiplies seemingly
at the cost of the creation of any other value. In his book on
the acceleration of time, *Chaos: Making a New Science,* James
Gleick sees this in another context when he notes the rise
and dominance of day trading in recent years. Day traders, a
powerful force in financial markets from the 1990s and almost
unheard of before that, do not pursue production schedules or
balance sheets; they do not analyse business plans or evaluate
company management, he notes. They stare at computer
screens, 'watching numbers flash by'.[16]

This development is so extreme that it almost does away
with the need to accept or question Marx's notion of exchange
and use value, once anathema to non-Marxists. Much of

financial capital creates no value at all, however defined. At least in this sense, Amin is right in claiming that the 'market invoked by conventional economists no longer exists. It is truly a farcical joke.'[17] In a related context, as Bauman notes, today '[t]he main sources of profits [...] tend to be [...] ideas rather than material objects'.[18] Actually, even here, we are not talking of ideas in the sense of Edison's inventions or Einstein's theory of relativity. We are talking of empty air, sheer liquid that flows without even planning on assuming shape: 'empty' numbers that have 'worth' only within the structure of abstract financial power that imbues them with 'worth', and not because of any exchange, trade, or production that they directly facilitate.

Amin provides a schema of what he calls 'modern (capitalist) polarization' that has appeared during the evolution of the capitalist mode of production.[19] It is useful as an analysis of capitalism, partly because—unlike some other Marxist accounts—it implicitly sees capitalism as both continuing and changing from c. 1500 to the present. Starting with the mercantilist form of capitalism, located by Amin (and, a bit differently, also by Karl Polanyi) in 1500–1800, we have a build-up to the Industrial Revolution that 'was fashioned by the hegemony of merchant capital in the dominant Atlantic centers, and by the creation of the peripheral zones (the Americas) whose function involved their total compliance with the logic of accumulation of merchant capital'.[20] This leads to the so-called *classical model*, which Amin correctly identifies as growing out of the Industrial Revolution and defining the basic forms of what we still largely consider capitalism (even though high capitalism or finance capitalism is not the same as this classical model). Amin points out that this model was based on the global structure of an industrialized or swiftly industrializing 'centre' and a periphery (Asia—except for Japan,

Africa, and Latin America) whose 'participation in the world division of labour took place [largely] via agriculture and mineral production'.[21] He notes that this important characteristic of 'polarization' was accompanied by a second equally significant one: the crystallization of core industrial systems as mediated through nation states, with the powerful (developed) nations being able to mediate better within and without their own borders.[22]

This gave way to what Amin calls the *post-war period*, and places this between 1945 and 1990. He points out that this period marked the progressive erosion of the two (above-mentioned) characteristics of the classical model of capitalism. Along with being a period of unequal and uneven industrialization of the 'peripheries'—enabled also by national liberation movements from within—the period was simultaneously 'one of the progressive dismantling of autocentric national production systems and their re-composition as constitutive elements of an integrated world production system'.[23] In simpler words, the globalizing economy of capitalism became increasingly independent of the social and political mechanisms of 'mediating' nation states. This double erosion, as Amin puts it, was the sign of a 'deepening of globalization', which arrived fully with what Amin simply terms the 'most recent period' and has become glaring from the 1990s onwards.

It is this decisive, cumulative change that many refer to as that of globalization. It is sometimes objected that capitalism has always been global, and that the current phase does not signify any difference of quality. But though I insist on the globalizing nature of capitalism, I have also quoted extensively to underline the qualitative changes that have taken place since the 1970s. The decade of the 1970s, though in many cases its effects start showing only in the 1980s, is not a mark of convenience. One can even specify a particular year as marking the initial shift:

The concomitance of the US deficit (leading to an excess of dollars available on the market) and the crisis of productive investment produced a mass of floating capital with no place to go. The choice of floating exchange rates in 1973 was therefore perfectly rational: it allowed this gigantic mass of floating capital to find an outlet in financial speculation. Today, *while world trade is valued at US $ 2 billion, international capital movements are estimated at US $ 50 billion!*[24] (Italics mine)

It is with the choice of floating exchange rates in 1973 that we begin to enter the phase of high (finance) capitalism, or 'globalization' as some call it, a development that then took more than a decade to spread and consolidate.

Changes in the Welfare States

One of the great compromises of the post-war period in the old colonizing nations—under the impetus of the Red threat, as well as the dominance of Social Democracy internally—was the one between employers and trade unions, with governments acting as midwives. This still structures the economic planning of nations like Denmark and Germany, though increasingly the old trade unions are seen as facilitating conflict-free working spaces for employers than protecting the rights of employees. This was a system that was worked out in an international system of classical capitalism, where national safeguards were put into place in most rich countries in order to derive the maximum benefits and to cut the drawbacks accruing from *international* capitalism.

It can even be seen as the liberal version of a communist compromise: the communist compromise, promoted by Lenin and Stalin against Trotsky, abandoned international 'revolution' for a 'national example' (as in the USSR). This was a compromise that ran against some Marxist understandings of capitalism and, it can be argued, ended in total failure, with the dissolution of the USSR and the movement to statist capitalism by China. Interestingly, one can see, in such cases, how xenophobia returns in exactly the phases when a group or nation becomes an obvious contender for power: for instance, the invasion scare stories and novels of the beginning of the twentieth century, which often featured the 'yellow peril', coincided with the rise of Japan and China, and similarly in recent years the media in UK and USA have been mixing justified criticism of the system in China with rhetoric that smacks of 'chinaphobia'. The USSR/ Russia is another example: after the 'russophobia' of the Cold War years, and following the dissolution of the USSR, Russia entered the good books of media discourse in the West, despite rampant corruption and crime, and it is only now, with Putin flexing his muscles regionally, that Russians are being painted with a phobic brush (as generically untrustworthy, not really European, dictatorial, unable to have 'real' democracy, etc.) once again. On the other hand, with Putin struggling to control Ukraine, one can also see how Russian media and official discourse has returned to the sort of West-phobic statements that marked the Soviet years.[25]

But to continue with the larger story, on the liberal side, in the old colonial nations of Europe, as well as in upcoming rich 'white' settler nations—pitiably imitated by less prosperous postcolonial nations—the social welfare compromise curtailed industrial conflict internally, by protecting ordinary citizens, while enabling businessmen to reap the benefits of international capitalism. But while the fall of the Berlin Wall dramatically illustrated the failure of the communist compromise, the fraying of the liberal compromise of welfare states has yet to be taken into account fully. This was the case even though by the 1980s, the signs were already there, and for obvious reasons: the lack of a democratic power system to manage social and political matters at the global level in a world of economic globalization.[26]

It is not even a question of 'maturity'; the world system worked on the basis of rich countries being protected with effective welfare states, and the rest of the world being open to 'free trade'. The functioning national welfare systems of the First World, constructed on the basis of old colonial exploitation and classical capitalist dominance, are not the exception, but a part of the unequal system of global capitalism. The rise of finance capitalism does not resolve this problem, as Amin notes,

The market of floating capital, which has dwarfed the first [goods and services] market since the 1970s, has only marginal interest in the Third World, although it should be noted that a major fraction of the capital accumulated in many areas of Latin America, Africa, and the Middle East is collected by this market, thanks to the liberalization and globalization of financial and banking systems (which East and South-East Asia, and India, are trying to resist). On the other hand, most of this capital seeks investment by roaming from one financial metropolis to another, only rarely paying a visit to Third World financial systems.[27]

Amin is partly incorrect here. As the Third World also contains financial metropolises—say, Mumbai—what exists now is a network of financial metropolises, of which far fewer (especially in ratio to the population) are situated in the Third World. The vast mass of floating capital mentioned by Amin circulates from metropolis to metropolis, passing hastily over the spaces (urban or rural) in between. In this context, it is important to stress that there exists a globalized metropolitan culture—some kinds of fiction and their privileged critical reception reflects this too—that cannot be situated simply along the First World/Third World or West/East axis.

Hence, aspects of new xenophobia also exist in highly 'capitalized' circles in the Third World. Take, for instance, the under-reported farmer suicides of India. According to the latest report of the National Crime Records Bureau, more than a quarter million impoverished and indebted farmers committed suicide in a period of 16 years in India.[28] This figure is shocking enough, but the real figure is much higher. These 256,913 suicides are only those registered as suicides by the police in a country where many deaths and births go unregistered, especially in the 'really backward' sections of society. Moreover, as Siddhartha Deb notes in *The Beautiful and the Damned*, because the authorities count as farmers only male heads of the household who have agricultural land registered in their names, the 'suicide figures do not include women, nor do they include the tens of millions who farm on land owned by other people'.[29] As interestingly, the states that receive the most 'positive' reports in certain sections of the international and national media—because they are seen as taking the right liberal steps to make India 'progress', such as removing state subsidies for seed purchase, etc. (strongly recommended at times by consulting bodies from countries like the USA which actually subsidize their own agriculture in a massive way)[30]—are also the states with some of the highest rates of farmer suicide.

The general apathy to the suicide and related deaths of farmers and their dependents, numbering anywhere between a quarter million to more than a million, in privileged circles of India or abroad is remarkable, especially if we put this figure next to the figures of major genocides, which seldom exceed these numbers. Evidently, one of the reasons the farmer suicides in India get less attention is that they are not seen as the result of violence or prejudice, which is not the case with the usual genocide. In some ways, the polite circles of Indians in Delhi indulge in a kind of abstract violence—and an evasion of its consequences—that can only be understood with reference to structures of new xenophobia, not of old xenophobia. A larger global example can be traced by noting the workings of pharmaceutical companies, as studied by Ben Goldacre in *Big Pharma: How Drug Companies Mislead Doctors and Harm Patients* and Jacky Law in *Big Pharma: Exposing the Global Healthcare Agenda*; in different ways, both books reveal how an abstract kind of discrimination, negotiated in sheer economic terms, impacts on and kills people who incidentally are often also the type persecuted by older forms of xenophobia. One can also look at the growing rift between the developed world and developing nations over climate change—with its human and natural tragedies more immediate in the developing world and its financial responsibilities increasingly shirked by the developed world[31]—along similar lines.

It is, however, also true that the 'spaces in between' in the West and/or the First World are often protected much better than their equivalents in the East and/or the Third World by either the greater dominance of the national economy, or an established welfare state system that shares in the relative dominance of First World and/or Western economies. Today, the welfare states of rich countries are being pressed by the contradictions of the above system. This is different from what mostly existed under classical capitalism, where national governments of rich countries could mediate a national compromise between labour and business, while leaving capital free to compete in other national spaces on dominant terms. This was so because capital was still largely petrified in commodities (and money) and depended on national and international trade. With money dissolving into free-floating finance capital—numbers mostly—national governments are now less able to control international finance and investment, and hence to assuage local labour, which nevertheless continues to wield the vote in these technically democratic countries.[32]

It is interesting how the discussion around immigrants, etc.— say, both the pro- and anti-multiculturalism schools—serves to obscure, and even distort, the real changes of globalization. For instance, only about 2 per cent of the world's population consists of actual migrants and refugees.[33] In contrast, floating capital—by definition global—is at least twenty times the value of actual trade, which can be national or global. In effect, the movement of people/labour under globalization is *insignificant* in comparison to the movement of capital and goods. This is something that the most conscientious economists recognize, but fear to stress today, as one can see in all the admirable work of Joseph Stiglitz, once the chief economist of the World Bank and today a critic from the side of basically pro-capitalism economics.[34]

By definition, this new globalization erodes the efficiency of economic management by nation states. However, it does not abolish their existence. Thus, it produces a new contradiction that, in my opinion, is insurmountable under high capitalism. The reason for this is that capitalism is more than just an economic (let alone a financial) system; its economy is inconceivable without a social and political dimension, which implies a state. Until recently, the expansion of capitalism was founded on the coincidence (especially in dominant and colonizing/ex-colonizing regions) between the space in which the reproduction of accumulation was determined and the space of its political and social management, as Bauman has observed; the interventions of the central nation states shaped the structure of the international system. Now, however, we have entered a new era characterized by a chasm between the globalized space of capitalism's economic management and the national space of its political and social management.[35]

A central argument of this book is a corollary of this widely accepted proposition: that globalization has marked a disjunction between the space of capitalism's economic management and the national space of its political and social management. In this sense, the rise of xenophobia in European welfare states is not just easy to understand (contrary to what some media 'experts' imply), but is also predicated on this change: the political and social management of capital, in a globalized world in which its economic management tends to slip outside the grasp of states, involves the control of not capital, but of people/labour. In this context, the political and social management of capital by nation states involves strategies that either encourage xenophobia or lead to paranoia among the citizens, regardless of what the ostensible position of the state might be on matters racial or religious. These contradictions are at the core of new forms of xenophobia.

Xenophobia and the Crisis of Advanced Welfare States

The early nexus between capitalism and the nation state has been widely documented. Giddens, for instance, states that the two have been 'intertwined' in their 'mutual development'.[36] However, Giddens, like most others, lets the matter rest there, and merely ends up suggesting a casual collaborative link between nation-statism and capitalism without exploring the dynamics of the matter. This fails to indicate how the two are linked.

As is obvious, nationalism had and has its advantages—and many of these accrete to the national bourgeoisie under a trade- and production-based mode of capitalism. Nationalism creates the half-true myth of a horizontal (and not vertical) division of society which obscures the fact that some continue to live at the cost of many. It constitutes the 'serfs' into 'free peasantry' which can defend the status quo better and can be 'freed' even further into the condition of workers with only their labour to sell; that is, it not only gets workers to *work*, but also gets them to *consume* on capitalist terms. Finally, it constitutes a state that while keeping 'order' in the nation also protects the national bourgeoisie from external threats (not least economic ones) to the best of its ability. The social welfare state is the ultimate outcome of this tendency, though not the only one.

The argument that First World capitalist states do not indulge in much economic protectionism was and is blind to the fact that their bourgeoisies are in such positions of strength that they stand to gain *more* by competing on 'equal terms' with other bourgeoisies.[37] This is a fact not lost on other bourgeoisies; witness the hamstrung attempts by a rightist party like the Bharatiya Janata Party to keep international *capitalists* out of India while trying to invite international *capital* into the country. On the other hand, wherever and whenever 'developed' nations risk competition on unfavourable terms (such as in the fields of agriculture and textiles), their governments obligingly 'call out the police and the military' (in George Bernard Shaw's words), or at least implement protectionist policies. The current global financial crisis is just another indication of this, if we bear in mind facts like this one:

when the 'Asian tiger' economies suffered a similar recession in the 1980s, First World nations and their international bodies urged them to let their banks sink and collapse on their own steam. However, the same First World governments have spent most of the past five years pumping capital into their own banks in order to keep them going.

The above observation does not mean that the state is a *creation* of nationalism. Anyone with even a rudimentary acquaintance with history knows that, in their various forms, states preceded nationalism by at least a couple of millennia. But while the state is not a creation of nationalism, the current 'universality' of states *is* a creation of nationalism and capitalism. Pre-capitalist societies could be organized in forms other than that of a state; pre-capitalist states could also contain diverse peoples, sometimes called 'nations'. However, the core theory of nationalism *insists* not only on a state, but also posits *one state for one nationality*. In cases where there is a reasonable chance of success—either due to numerical strength, economic growth, geographical factors, or international support—this assumption leads to demands for independence, as in the case of India/Pakistan from the Raj, Bangladesh from Pakistan, or, more recently, a number of 'new countries' in East Europe. But if success and support are seriously in doubt, the word used is 'autonomy'—as in Kashmir currently and in Kosovo recently. If on the one side of this equation we have the liberal freedom of the market, on the other side—given political and economic developments—we have the socialist structure of the welfare state. In rich countries, they have gone together, the USA being an ideological exception, despite Thomas Paine and its own early history,[38] partly because of its domineering position in the capitalist market. As the bulwark of 'free' capitalism, the USA has been more sceptical of social welfare. This has allowed the other rich capitalist states (from Canada to Denmark, which troop along, whatever their internal differences may be, on the wide global highway policed by the USA) to develop varieties of social-welfarism that somewhat regulate market and labour internally in the nation. But this welfarism was not just made possible by the relative colonial prosperity of most of these countries; it is sustained only by the wealth available from 'free' capitalism, policed by USA and NATO, which was always international and is now 'global'.

This is all fine up to a point in these spaces, the point where capital *frees* itself significantly from trade/money and hence human-based productivity. It is this point that was reached in the phase, variously located around the 1980s to 1990s, when the word 'globalization' started replacing the word 'capitalism' as an index of our present world structure. Once this happens, as indicated above, the capitalist (advanced/ developed) welfare state is faced with a greater contradiction than a largely liberal capitalist state such as the USA. As Asa Briggs notes when discussing the rise of the welfare state in the historical context, unemployment, as a social contingency, 'is a product of industrial society, and it is unemployment more than any other social contingency which has determined the shape and timing of modern welfare legislation'.[39] If so, globalization—with its highly abstract, free-floating capital and its correspondingly unequal flow of global capital and global labour—will inevitably create, particularly so in the absence of global political structures to address the problem, pronounced xenophobic sentiments in national circles, and new xenophobic forms of power and prejudice. Hence, it is not surprising that my illustrations of new forms of xenophobia are drawn largely from those very welfare states of Europe that take pride in having overcome the old forms of xenophobia, which still seem to recur more often not just in the Third World or in developing nations, but also in the socio-economically uneven USA. This is not to be particularly critical of the developed welfare states of Europe; there is every chance that just as the forms of old xenophobia spread internationally with the spread of production-based capitalism, the forms of new xenophobia will also be diligently copied in the circles of high capitalism and its legislators elsewhere. One can already see it happening, as I indicate with some examples in this book, in high capitalist, mostly metropolitan, circles in the USA and in India, and it has similar versions in other countries (and privileged cities) with significant capital investment and circulation.

In short, with the above sequence of changes and unresolved contradictions, we enter a world where *the prosperity of rich welfare states depends on the ability of their capital to circulate freely.* This prosperity structures and finances the very welfare state that keeps such nations socially stable. But while these states require capital to move freely, they cannot really permit the other side of the liberal capitalist equation: free movement of labour. As they cannot theoretically have only the one and not the other, labour is increasingly prevented from entering these spaces—not as labour, but in other abstract ways. The tendency, inherent in capitalism and modernity, to define 'monsters' in abstract ways takes a further and decisive turn; unlike the abstraction that had been called upon to justify the categorization of visible or deviously hidden physical/material differences, now we have abstraction that in itself can be contrasted against any reiteration of the non-abstract.

Among other things, this leads to legislation and perceptions that are very different from those of old xenophobia at times. Indeed, given the need not to see labour as a working body, but to prevent its entry *in the abstract,* as well as the highly abstract nature of high capitalism, this leads to a sort of highly abstract xenophobia, which I consider an element of the new xenophobia. The 'good'—like abstract capital flying free of labour, goods, and even money now—is increasingly seen as under attack by manifestations of the physical/material 'bad'.

3

RACISM, NATIONALISM, AND NAZISM

I have highlighted how old xenophobia depended (and depends) on physical and material indicators of difference. But this says very little, especially if one puts it next to my other statement: that I do not use old xenophobia to refer to all kinds of xenophobia in the past. I use it to refer to xenophobia as framed and expressed in the centuries of colonialism-based early capitalism and production-based classical capitalism. In what ways did these centuries, with their interlinked power equations of colonization and early or classical capitalism, determine the forms and nature of old xenophobia? Surely we have to document this before we can go on with our study of new xenophobia? One way to do so is to examine the three 'isms' commonly associated with outbreaks of old xenophobia: racism, nationalism, and Nazism.

There are some obvious similarities between racism and nationalism, despite their differences. This is most readily accessed in Nazism, which combined nationalism with racism. One major similarity is the existence of certain assumptions that, both in racism and in nationalisms, tend to 'naturalize' various ideological underpinnings with reference to a hoary past. For instance, racism is often based on pseudo-theories of tribal and genetic inheritances going back many centuries.

Nationalism—especially, but not only in its volk incarnations—depends on similarly vague but powerful bids to naturalize itself with reference to an ancient, and often a physical, inheritance of difference. Both were combined in glaringly obvious ways in the Nazi rewording of Aryan-hood.

This is a characteristic of old xenophobia. Old xenophobia naturalizes itself by referring to a hoary past and to 'natural' (biological, evolutionary, genetic) elements, but these elements are always crafted and defined in the present. In general terms too, these are problematic, whether it is the assumption of total strangeness, or of given difference, or of natural fear. If one were to write an account of such popular constructions of xenophobia as a short history, one would end up highlighting tribal elements of difference and emotional elements of bonding. I have already indicated that the former is misleading. Just as misleading is the claim that we only empathize or sympathize with one of our own. This begs the question of the historically determined constructions of 'our own', and hence of self and other. It is also, as Terry Eagleton notes, simply not true: we can feel very little about those next to us and get very worked up about distant people and faraway events. Xenophobia is thus not an unavoidable *natural*, almost bodily, reaction; it is always, to some extent or the other, constructed.

And yet the myth of 'natural' xenophobia is essential to what I have called old xenophobia. In all its more common versions—those of racism (including anti-Semitism), extreme nationalism (ethnic or linguistic), and in the political forms of Nazism—old xenophobia insists on a clear and given *body* of difference, even as the difference becomes progressively abstract under capitalism. It suggests a direct pedigree extending far back into the past, in terms of tribal-ethnic definitions of nationhood or biological definitions of races, etc. This pedigree was constructed, effectively, in the eighteenth and nineteenth centuries, and shaped by structures of early, classical, and production-based capitalism. I will illustrate this by focusing on slavery, racism, nationalism, and Nazism, which is each indelibly associated in our memories and history books with some of the worst outbreaks of old xenophobia.

Slavery and Racism

Contrary to what is sometimes assumed, one cannot talk of capitalism—or could not until its late twentieth-century manifestations—without taking into account an institution that, as Adam Smith realized very early, is basically antithetical to the logic of capitalism. This is slavery. However, like capitalism or any other long-lasting socio-economic, symbolic–materialist construction (such as 'religion', for instance), 'slavery' is a dangerous term to use. Because it suggests a commonality across the ages (the physical control of other human bodies), it is often easy to forget that its aspects have also altered with social, cultural, and economic changes over the centuries. What was slavery in ancient Greece was not necessarily the same as slavery in seventeenth-century Europe; what was slavery in fourteenth-century Turkey was not necessarily the same as slavery in eighteenth-century Jamaica. And yet, it was all slavery to the extent that it involved a system of sale/control and, in due course, 'ownership' of other human bodies.

In his book, Steven Pinker notes that until recently slavery was the rule rather than the exception, 'upheld in the Hebrew and Christian Bibles [and ...] justified by Plato and Aristotle as a natural institution that was essential to civilized society.

So-called democratic Athens in the time of Pericles enslaved 35 percent of its population, as did the Roman Republic.'[1] From there, Pinker moves on and again notes, with absolute accuracy, that 'between the 16th and 19th centuries at least 1.5 million Africans died in transatlantic slave ships, chained together in stifling filth-ridden holds' and the ones who survived mostly met a fate of unimaginable exploitation and brutality.[2] Compared to this history of slavery, Pinker says, we live in a world that is almost free of slavery, largely thanks to a mass movement against chattel slavery that arose as late as the eighteenth century and succeeded to a large extent only from the middle of the nineteenth century. At worst, slavery exists as a clandestine practice, and this was unimaginable just two centuries ago.[3]

But what is more relevant to our study is not as much the continuity in the theory of slavery—the fact that it involves the direct control of a human body by other human bodies—as the wide divergences in its practice across time. If this explains why there were major slave dynasties in mediaeval India,[4] Egypt,[5] and Turkey, it also explains the tragedy of the *Zong* (which we shall encounter later in this chapter) in the eighteenth century and the New York Public Library exhibition of January 2013, curated by Sylviane Diouf for Black History Month—Africans in India: From Slaves to Generals and Rulers.

All of ancient and mediaeval slavery was greatly varied. As one scholar notes, '"Greco-Roman" actually covers a number of very different slave systems [...]. These in turn were subject to considerable change over time.'[6] In general, both in Greece and Rome, slaves were acquired in various ways: sale in the market, debt enslavement, warfare, kidnapping, and perhaps child exposure. There is 'little surviving evidence of slave breeding (or slave families)' in ancient Greece.[7] Slaves in Greece were involved in agricultural work and mining, but they were also used for artisanal work and business (and sometimes allowed great autonomy). While the evidence of plays such as the comedies of Aristophanes suggests that slaves, as always, were vulnerable to what we would today call physical abuse by their masters, we also know that Greece and Rome had laws protecting their slaves. Slaves were also not racially marked—there were Greek and Roman slaves—and they could be freed in various ways.

As was the case in Greece, Rome, and all over the world, slavery was indigenous in Asia and Africa.[8] This means, among other things (also, as encountered above, in the case of Greece and Rome), that the imbrications of racism and slavery, which was a dominant feature in nineteenth-century Europe and in European settler countries, was not a significant factor. Slaves could be 'outsiders', but this was not necessarily the case, as we have also seen in ancient Greece and Rome. Scholars have noted that in the Indian Ocean 'world', 'the majority of people entering slavery [...] probably did so through debt', as enslavement was legally enforced for defaulting debtors and their relatives in these regions.[9] Again, both in Asia and Africa, natural disasters could impoverish families to the extent that family members were sold 'into bondage to enhance the chances of survival of both the individual sold and the remaining family members'.[10]

Scholars have suggested that when we talk of 'slavery' in pre-colonial Africa, we often confuse it with other social relationships, and that, in this sense, 'slavery' is a misleading term. This highlights an important aspect of all discussions of early slavery (and a point that is essential to an understanding of the physicality of old xenophobia): that slavery was only one kind of body ownership in a range of forms of bodily servitude, ranging from some forms of marriage and debt repayment to various kinds of human pawnship.

It is this perception that I have been aiming at: slavery not only had different forms, but it was also itself one of the forms in which the human body was constituted and exchanged. Obviously, in barter-based and agricultural societies, the human body was a direct and evident source of value. The human body was not just the source of wealth to begin with; it was also wealth, and could be treated as such: almost all known societies, for instance, allowed parents to dispose of their children in marriage, for indenture, etc., at least until the children reached maturity. In the case of societies where capital formation was non-existent or low, the human body not only exchanged, but could also be exchanged itself. While the abstraction of money—also as early (and limited) capital—impacted on these bodies, it could not erase them substantially. The body was, in some ways, one of the monies of pre-capitalistic societies, and it was exchanged not just through slavery, but also through various other forms, including some that have survived in altered shapes, such as marriage, parentage, and adoption.

Highlighting the various monies that preceded the creation of a universal national currency as late as the nineteenth century, Viviana A. Zelizer quotes Marcel Mauss to the effect that money is 'essentially a social fact' and notes that '[t]he earmarking of money is thus a social process: money is attached to a variety of social relations rather than to individuals'.[11] In many ways, the human body has also, legally until recently, been used as 'currency'. In societies where wealth is inevitably and directly created by human labour and not free-floating capital, it seems that control—and sale—of human bodies was logical. Slavery, along with marriage, was one of the modes of doing so, legally.

It is not that marriage was the only other institution that depended on control of the human body and its exchange between powerful (mostly male) members of societies; all social relationships, ranging from serfdom, bondage, and various types of servitude to parentage and family relations, could be ranked, until recently, along a scale of direct physical marking and control. This has changed largely only in spaces that are structured by capitalism, as indicated by Marx's double-edged praise of the bourgeoisie.[12]

Kecia Ali's *Marriage and Slavery in Early Islam* illustrates a relevant aspect of slavery in early times, across overlapping cultures:

There are critical similarities and vital differences among Roman, Jewish, and Islamic laws regulating marriage and slavery. The similarities illuminate the broader context of the ancient Near East and [the] Mediterranean. All use <u>terms related to 'acquisition' or 'sale' for some forms of marriage</u>, but the rabbinic *kinyan*, acquisition, is central, while to Roman, *coemptio*, a fictive sale, is marginal. The archaic <u>Roman form of marriage known as *manus* refers to the husband's 'hand' as a representation of his power</u>, as do the Muslim terms *yad* (hand) and *milk al-yamîn* <u>(ownership by the right hand), which refer to control over certain marital rights</u> (by a husband or father) and to slave ownership, often concubinage.[13] (Italics in original; underlining mine)

As the extracts underlined by me indicate, there was a clear theoretical overlap between the kind of exchange of body that took place under marriage and the kind that took place as slavery. This was not 'indicative of doctrinal borrowing', but 'rather of a broader culture of legal understandings growing out of hierarchical social structures'[14]—and, I would add, of a social hierarchy where power was still imposed physically on the body, as source and measure of wealth, as 'goods' to be bartered that, with the rise of money economies, also came to be seen as a kind of money to be exchanged. Hence, not only slave prices, etc., but also dowries, bride money, etc. As Ali notes, 'premodern Muslims were typical rather than unique in having both patriarchal marriage and slaveholding'.[15]

Ali makes another vital point when she illustrates that marriage in these times did not suddenly subjugate an *independent* woman, but all women and 'subordinate men' were *already* part of a shifting hierarchy of 'kin control'.[16] Hence, what has to be imagined is a network of physically determined controls, all centring on the body, along different lines: for the free woman, this would stretch from childhood to death, with marriage being an aspect of it; for the subordinate male, this would stretch from various kinds of servitude (familial, parental, kinship-, tribe-, guild-, or society-based), with slavery being arguably an extreme aspect of it.[17]

Gail Labovitz provides a similar model for understanding the relationship between wives, slaves, and other possessions in rabbinic thought—where, too, women in their bodies were seen as 'ownable'.[18] It was not just that in many early societies—I am using the Muslim context as a broad example—ideas of bonded servitude and slavery were inseparable from that of marriage (as, also, in the Hindu tradition of the wife being her husband's *dasa* or slave/servitor, undergirded repeatedly in the ancient epics). It is more important to understand that all of these (marriage, slavery, servitude, kinship, etc.) were part of an interlocking grid of property rights and bodily rights. The two could not be separated from each other in the absence of an instrument of power, like capital, which logically need not have a bodily existence. Extensive monetization, with its accumulating logic of capital, pointed in that direction for centuries, but it enabled the 'freeing' of bodies only from the eighteenth century onwards, only when modern capitalism assumed coherent and persistent shape.

The rise of monetary economies and their consolidation with early capitalism was to change all this, slowly and sporadically for centuries and extensively, with the consolidation of capitalism, from the eighteenth century onwards. By the nineteenth century, the slave was no longer part of a complex and graded—though, of course, exploitative—sequence of social relations, which, in effect, included everyone. This explains, for instance, the European/ized inability in the nineteenth century to understand such mediaeval Muslim practices as inheritance laws that gave preference to the favourite slave over 'blood relations' and bestowed legitimacy on the children of concubines from their masters. This entire spectrum of social relations no longer existed, having been destroyed as much by monetary economy and incipient capitalism as by racism (born from the nature of colonial successes to an extent). It is, then, that slavery is revealed as the equivalent of 'social death', in the words of Orlando Patterson, and anti-slavery becomes a pressing intellectual position also on the part of the 'free'. The two went hand-in-hand. The reduction of the slave from a subordinate status and a medium of exchange/ value, in a network of such relations of power and exchange, to just mere goods and, as we shall see, an expression of capital was essential to the fight for the human rights of the slave. It is in the light of this *reduction* of the slave that we also need to understand the nature of the *atrocities* of the slave trade of colonization and early capitalism: while far more slaves than Europeans were settled in America in the eighteenth century, the black population lagged behind the white due to the atrocious living and working conditions of the slaves, structured by institutionalized racism.[19]

Racism imbued slavery with abstract moral and cultural significance in the wake of monetized economies; 'difference' (obvious or hidden, real or imagined) was not just a physical fact now, but a moral, cultural, and even civilizational attribute, which justified the maltreatment of the stranger (or the slave). Just as the physical difference of monsters was increasingly abstracted into moral, social, and cultural differences, the enslavement of people was increasingly justified, in the eighteenth and nineteenth centuries, not with reference to the inheritance of physical and material differences or divine curses (which mark a people), but with a reworking of these corporal elements in moral, social, cultural, and scientific terms.

Social Darwinism, vital to nineteenth-century racism, illustrates this best as it brought abstract and sublimated social and political factors into seemingly 'solid' biology while appearing to do the reverse. Social Darwinism was 'not simply the importation of a biological doctrine into sociology. It was Darwinian biology that had previously imported into biology a sociological doctrine (that of bourgeois political economy).'[20] Pichot illustrates that the Darwinian version of natural selection as an explanation of biological evolution was not a revolutionary break from religion (instead, it was one evolutionary theory among others already in circulation), as it is often portrayed even today, nor was it sustained by the evidence in The Origin of Species (which does not contain a single example of evolution explained in this way), nor, finally, was it scientifically coherent or convincing before the 1910s (with the development of genetics, etc.). Its success in the second half of the nineteenth century was thus not due to these factors. Instead, Pichot points out, it provided a biological rationale that was ideologically acceptable to the bourgeoisie. For instance, it marked a movement away from the aristocratic idea of heredity ('blue blood', which was not as much a matter of genetics as of inherited titles and family name, and hence a perpetuation of a social order in which everyone had a fixed place) to the bourgeois idea of a meritocracy: Social Darwinism [...] introduced into bourgeois meritocracy a heredity that was genuinely biological and not at all symbolic. Meritocracy saw the triumph of the fittest, and Social Darwinism explained this triumph by a hereditary biological superiority, recognition of which was the key to progress.[21]

It is important to understand this transmogrification of the physical and material basis of aristocracy—as classes and individuals with their apportioned state in society, determined partly by physical–biological and partly by socio-material heredity—to the meritocracy of the bourgeoisie, which is at the same time more abstract and more narrowly 'physical–biological' in its understanding of heredity. The abstraction of capital and property is rooted, perforce, in a physicality that, almost inevitably, leads to racism. This is racism as a system (not the prior collocation of prejudices), both 'scientific' and socio-political, which inherently explains and justifies the 'meritocracy' of the bourgeoisie with little or no reference to the new enabling system of power: capital and property accruing through capital.

This abstraction-rooted-in-the-physical was essential to bourgeois ideological self-understanding, which needed to reprocess the physical base of slavery with the cultural factors of institutionalized, systemic 'racism' that had been brought into being (many centuries after slavery per se) by colonization and early capitalism. It helped to hide the deep imbrications of early capitalism with slavery as a source of capital accumulation, rather than a particularly oppressive aspect of rigid social relations.

The 1781 slave genocide on the ship *Zong* provides just one stark account of this. The *Zong* was a ship bought in Africa, by the captain of another ship, and chartered and sent to Africa by some merchants in Liverpool, then a major centre of the triangular slave trade. The captain had appointed his ship's doctor, Luke Collingwood, as the new captain of the *Zong*, which set sail with its cargo of 440 slaves from Africa on 6 September 1781. In his excellent study *Specters of the Atlantic*, Ian Baucom points out that the Liverpool merchants had neither seen the *Zong* nor the slaves purchased on their behalf. The slaves were bought, as was the custom, on credit and paid for with 'promissory notes' to be redeemed after a period of time on their sale in another continent, and hence undergirded by a capitalized system of insurance.[22]

Most of these long-confined and now-ailing slaves—already turned into commodities under a finance system in which the slave's value preceded and did not follow or coincide with exchange—were massacred, by being handcuffed and drowned off the coasts of Jamaica, on the orders of Captain Collingwood. Captain Collingwood had, just two days before ordering the massacre, turned back from a sighting of Jamaica, later claiming that he had mistaken it for another island; the massacre, which went on for a number of days, was continued on the captain's orders even though scarcity of water, a reason given for the 'disposal' of the slaves, no longer remained a factor (because of rainfall during which the crew collected eleven days' worth of drinking water).[23]

What is revealing in this case is that the massacre on the *Zong* became a legal issue in England not on what we would call 'human rights' grounds, but on financial ones: were the owners entitled to collect the insurance money, for Captain Collingwood believed and claimed that he had ordered the drowning of the ailing slaves to protect the financial interests of the owners, or, more correctly, investors in Liverpool? It was not slaves (as people and even as goods) who were insured, but their abstract value, as capital that had not even been paid out as money by the investors in Liverpool or by the purchasers in America. Here, obviously, we have moved beyond the transformation of slaves from goods to be exchanged—perhaps common to all kinds of slavery—to commodities, which is a feature only of slavery in the phases of capitalism, however early. The slaves on the *Zong* were not just commodities to be sold or exchanged:

The genius of insurance, the secret of its contribution to finance capitalism, is its insistence that the real test of something's value comes not at the moment it is made or exchanged but at the moment it is lost or destroyed. In a pure commodity culture (if there ever was such a thing), that value would cease to exist the moment the commodity ceased to exist.[24]

The slaves on the *Zong* are very different, in this sense, from the early slaves we have encountered. There are two main reasons for this difference: (a) the rise of finance capital as a value prior to, and independent of, the commodity or goods of the slave's body, so that the legal question is not that of the destruction of the slave's body, but the restoration of the value credited between investors and prospective buyers via bankers; and (b) the relative 'liberation' of other bodies from physical constraint within a new social structure, increasingly enabled by capitalism, in which the slave, nevertheless, remained physically controlled. This latter point becomes clearer if we notice the degree to which our current (and correct) repugnance from, say, wife-beating and child-thrashing arise as a concerted social sentiment also in the eighteenth and nineteenth centuries.

The physicality of old xenophobia shares this element of the slavery of early capitalism; it registers the real or imagined difference of the stranger's body not in the sense in which early slavery inserted the slave's body into a larger control structure of embodied social relations, but in *the later sense of a moral or intellectual excuse with which to justify and perpetuate a basically non- and pre/quasi-capitalist exploitation of the body of another human.* This physicality has to be identified: Jews and Turks need 'beaked' noses; 'negroes' have to be thick-lipped and jet black; Moors have to be lascivious; Indians have to be effeminate; etc. In some instances, as was the case with most Jews in Europe in the early twentieth century, when the difference cannot be naturally identified, it was administratively imposed: Jews were segregated and forced to wear signs of identification.

Racism, in this sense, is a recent creation: here we are talking of not ethnic prejudices, but an institutionalization of these prejudices along pseudo-scientific and pseudo-moral lines of 'race theory'. Race theory 'not only assumes the existence of distinct, identifiable races each with its own separate "essence" or "character", but it also presupposes a hierarchy of difference'.[25] This bolus of fact and fiction is sustained by an intermingling of physical signs of difference with moral attributes, which, in turn, sanctify differential treatment of 'superior' and 'inferior' races. The physical, biological, and material difference of old xenophobia, in other words, comes to buttress an abstract scaffolding of moral, ideational, and intellectual attributes. It becomes necessary for that reason, and not because, as was the case with early slavery, it is just an aspect of a physical network of power relations. The border/contact zone of old power structures of slavery, with the greater abstraction of early and classical capitalism, is the space that gives us racism—as a systemic and often institutionalized bio-moral-political construct distinct from prior tribal and other prejudices.

There is obviously a difference between a structure or structures in which bodies are controlled (and even negated in extremis) because the operation of power is primarily physical and material, on the one hand, and a structure or structures in which (some) bodies have already been negated by the highly abstract power of capital, on the other hand. '[T]he goal of racism is dominance', stresses Memmi in his study of racism.[26] Or as he elaborates later in the book, racism implies 'a theory of biological differences' (drawing upon the ideas of 'the apologists of slave trade and for colonization') and it consists of 'the generalized and final assigning of values to real or imaginary differences, to the accuser's benefit and at the victim's expense, in order to justify the former's own privileges and aggression'.[27] That, of course, is also what made racism such an important element of old xenophobia, for, as argued throughout this book, xenophobia is always about power. This does not change, at least in recent centuries, with a shift in the nature of capitalism, as Nazism illustrated in the twentieth century. Nazism rose in a phase of classical or industrial capitalism which was significantly different from the kind of early (plantation and colonial-industrial) capitalism that used slavery as part of a systematic discourse of empowering racism for ruling sections of white Europeans and colonists. Nazism also built on a largely consolidated history (by the early twentieth century) of nationalism in what we now call First World states. And yet, like racist-slavery, Nazism was less about people and more about power, in a particular kind of capitalist world.

Nationalisms and Nazism

In extreme versions, as exemplified by Nazism, nationalisms do not differ much from racism. Both require a kind of naturalization with reference to a hoary past, as well as various 'given' (or inherited) physical and material indicators of difference. This is obvious enough in the case of volk nationalism, or was so in recent versions, before high capitalism impacted significantly on some notions of volk. But one can show that it was also the case, though less obviously, in extreme versions of linguistic nationalism.

Post-1789 French nationalism was, as E.J. Hobsbawn has shown in *Nations and Nationalism since 1780*, largely linguistically defined—though only 50 per cent of all Frenchmen spoke French in 1789 and only about 13 per cent spoke it 'correctly'. However, if one were willing to learn French, one could achieve the status of a French citizen. This contrasted with the other (later) tendency, the conservative one to which the term 'nationalism' was first applied, often on the basis of some perceived 'ethnic' or tribal communality.[28] According to this tendency, one's nationality was a bio-cultural inheritance, an aspect that, one could claim, goes back to prior and ancient notions of the tribe, now transposed, with intellectual and actual violence, on a trans-tribal and non-tribal concept like the 'nation'. This conception of national identity has been dominant in, for example, Germany, where nationality depended on belonging to the volk. Linguistic nationalisms, in this sense, use a less physical definition of the stranger than volk nationalisms, with their roots in pseudo-scientific theories of race and ethnicity, tend to employ. But the violent extirpation and imposition of 'strange' languages, in the name of national identity, which often overlaps with a perceived difference between the groups concerned, has also been put to obviously xenophobic uses.[29] In both cases—linguistic or volk—nationalism means the construction, contestation, and development of a unified 'national' identity by one or more ascendant power-groups, at the cost of elements that could not or would not be assimilated and groups that had to be disempowered.

What I have referred to as old xenophobia often bears the mark of this contestation and development; hence, the peoples killed for being ethnically (which often means linguistically) different in various places, ranging from Indonesia and Sri Lanka to former Yugoslavia. Language (or interchangeably 'culture'), in such cases, is the abstraction that covers physical—'ethnic'— differences or replaces them, in a way similar to the manner in which the abstractions of a systemic, Social Darwinist 'racism' came to stand in for, and replace, the physical and material embedding of prior structures of power.

Nationalism, either in its linguistic versions or in its volk versions, or as a combination of both, consists of the attempt to create general categories mostly on the grounds of naturalized differences, and this obviously includes the categories of 'nationals' and 'aliens'. Hence, xenophobia, as it might or might not have existed in the ancient Greek city states, should not be equated with old xenophobia, which, as we have seen, is impacted upon by a very different history of power (largely racist slavery), identity (nationalism), and economy (capitalism). Burbank and Cooper observe that for 'many [ancient and mediaeval] empires, loyalty, not likeness, was the goal'.[30] Moreover, under both volk and linguistic nationalisms, a stranger could be a far more abstract entity; in some versions, the fact that he may not be physically identifiable as a stranger made/makes no difference to his exclusion. But as this difference was predicated upon the stranger being strange and unknown and alien, old xenophobia often imposed or insisted on imposing the mark of this difference on the 'outsider', as Jews realized in Nazi Germany and Czarist Russia. Even as the reasons for xenophobic fear and hatred become more abstract under the impact of capitalism, old xenophobia kept/keeps insisting on the need to physically tag a stranger as different in her body/being.

Nationalist xenophobia is often based on contorted and hamstrung rivalries between regional, national, and international bourgeoisie, further distorted by the fact that the top layers of capitalist society are part of a global society by virtue of their power to move their capital globally, with its other members living/located nationally at least much of the time, with houses, jobs, salaries, loans tied down to a region or a nation. But such nationalist xenophobia still belonged (and belongs) to the category of old xenophobia because the 'national' capitalist classes, until the rise of high capitalism, were mostly tied to national labour, national production, and even, in most cases, national currency. All these become easier to examine—because they were so grossly exaggerated—in the case of Nazism.

'Need we recall that to [erroneously] base politics on biology is characteristic of Nazism?' Pichot asks in *The Pure Society*.[31] The ways in which the Nazis deployed selected aspects of Darwinism and developed their own kind of Social Darwinism as a rationale for their ideology have been variously documented. Not all of it was clearly worked out by their ideologues, and little of it had to do with Darwinism, as similar ideas were in the air in European and Europeanized societies in the second half of the nineteenth century and the first half of the twentieth century. Instead, such entangled ideas and beliefs often seeped into Nazi discourse as 'naturally' as in this extract (which can be replaced by similar statements by Nazi ideologues) from a speech by Himmler in October 1943:

For the SS man, one principle must apply absolutely: we must be honest, decent, loyal, and comradely to members of our own *blood*, and to no one else. What happens to the Russians, the Czechs, is totally indifferent to me. [...] Whether other races live well or die of hunger is only of interest to me insofar as we need them as *slaves* for our culture [...] We have arisen through the *law of selection*. We have *selected* from the average of our people. [...] The moment we forget the *law of the racial foundation* of our people, *the law of selection and severity* with regards to ourselves, then the *germ* of death will lie within us. [...] For that reason, it is our duty to remember our principle: *blood, selection, severity.*[32] (Italics mine)

Here we find the bogus admixture of the biological and the political by which the scientifically dubious Darwinian notions of 'natural selection' and 'survival of the fittest'[33] are put to the political use of institutionalizing a certain hierarchy of (racist and nationalist) power, which is perhaps the main defining feature of Nazism and related ideologies.

Ideas of social struggle, competition, and selection/ survival were already rampant in the nineteenth century; they formed the backbone of attempts by the bourgeoisie to justify their own privileges and advantages, either vis-à-vis the 'undeserving' or 'lazy' poor, 'hysterical' women, or 'decadent' or 'primitive' colonized peoples. As noted earlier, Pichot stresses that the Darwinian concepts of natural selection and survival of the fittest extended and reinforced the then current sociological thinking by reworking the notion of aristocratic inheritance in the bourgeois terms of a hereditary meritocracy. The aristocratic concept of heredity—blue blood—contained the notion of biological descent as part of a much broader social dimension: its 'decisive fact was not the transmission of genes ("aristocratic genes"), but that of a name and a title, and the perpetuation of a social order in which each person, whether aristocrat or commoner, had a place from which they were not to move'.[34] It also did not involve a conflation of biological and social superiority. Hereditary aristocracy was not a matter of genes to the extent that it presupposed an evolutionary superiority; it was common knowledge that consanguineous marriage among the aristocracy ended up accumulating hereditary defects, reflected in common reports of haemophilia in English and Russian royal families and in the 'terrible secrets' of great houses in eighteenth-century Gothic literature.

The process by which ideas of struggle, survival, selection, and competition were borrowed from the social and political spheres, passed through biology and returned as Social Darwinism enabled a conflation of heredity and bourgeois meritocracy: 'Meritocracy saw the triumph of the fittest, and Social Darwinism explained this triumph by a hereditary biological superiority, recognition of which was the key to progress.'[35]

But unlike Darwinists, Nazi ideologues were not talking of the individuals, regardless of their stress on physical and biological elements. Nazis (and related ideologues) had given a revealing twist to classical Darwinism, as Pichot notes. In Nazi thinking, individual survival is overshadowed by, and is secondary to, volk or 'racial' survival. This was not the case with Darwin or even Darwinian genetics; orthodox Darwinism, for instance, saw success in competition in terms of the individual's ability to leave behind the maximum number of descendants. Nazi biology, however, develops the idea of the individual as totally subordinate to the 'race' or volk, whose survival can demand the extinction of the individual. The Nazi concept of volk as being larger than the individuals who constitute it is encapsulated in texts by various Nazi ideologues, such as the Nazi biologist Otmar von Verschuer's *Manuel d'eugénique et d'hérédité humaine*.[36] In these texts, the conjoining of the biological and the 'spiritual', 'blood' and volk, etc., worked both ways: by posing an unproved and faulty 'spiritual' unity with reference to physical 'biology', and by undermining the individual biological specimen with reference to this larger and spurious volk spirituality.

What is interesting, from the perspective of the notion of xenophobia, is how such texts—directly or indirectly, advertently or inadvertently involved in the actual butchery of Jews, Gypsies, and others by the Nazis in the twentieth century (as Lindqvist notes)—begin to depict not just a difference, but also an *eradication* of difference in the name of a largely bogus universality or a largely abstract ideal (volk or 'race' or 'ethnicity'). In this sense, we already have an often-obscured movement away from 'tribal' notions of difference. The creation of the body of this particular stranger is predicated on the creation of the universal or ideal/abstract 'us' (volk); actually, the latter predicates the extermination of the particular stranger.

What is also interesting in this set of discourses—and we shall see this developed further under new xenophobia—is the movement towards the creation of the stranger as a repugnant body (monstrous *brute*, in that sense, too), while the universal 'us' is an abstract, almost ethereal, construct ('human being'); the body of the 'Aryan' is in proportion, ordered, perfect, regulated, perfumed, and hence, again, almost on the verge of entering the ethereal. It is not just a body, but an ideal body.

However, the body of the stranger—this strange, odious, deformed, abnormal, dirty body—is brutish also in the sense that it exists outside the paradigms of such physical duality, or as its contradiction or lacunae. As we have seen with vampires, among others, the physicality of this stranger is essential to its difference from the increasingly abstracted 'nation', volk, etc.; this very physicality needs to be eradicated, and its extermination is predicated upon the fact that this physicality can never belong within our increasingly abstract/ideal body of belonging in its difference. We are no longer just in the realm of different tribal totems or tattoos. The 'brutes' were constructed in words (and minds), but always exterminated or exiled in the body throughout most of the classical capitalist/colonial enterprise.

It is this that we were to encounter in Europe again, with Jews and Gypsies, as well as other 'undesirables' (political, such as communists, and social, such as homosexuals) herded into concentration camps. Once again, most of the people who perished in such concentration camps were considered 'inferior' and encouraged to disappear; their relationship to civilized space was that of 'dirt', as suggested earlier. In this sense, what happened to Jews in Hitler's concentration camps was the same as what happened to Hereros, around three decades earlier, in von Trotha's camps: the German General von Trotha pushed the indigenous Hereros out into an African desert, causing most of them to die of starvation and thirst.[37]

Nationalist-racist xenophobia is the most obvious and extreme version of old xenophobia, as it is based on elaborate theories of physically visible difference, which nevertheless serve purposes that are far more abstract. To identify it with 'tribal' xenophobia is to make a mistake because changing socio-economic circumstances always impinge on the creation of the stranger-to-be-feared, as well as the possible enactments of this fear. One way to understand this is to look at Nazi concentration camps or at the pre-Nazi obsession with physical culture that was taken to such extremes by Nazism. Various methods and exercises, as well as a whole repertoire of 'physical culture', were developed not just as part of a general 'health consciousness', but also as an aspect of a race and volk ideology, which differentiated between peoples in the body as well as in the 'essence' through the means of the highly normative, increasingly abstract/ideal 'perfect' body of the 'Aryan'.[38]

The body was no longer *just* a body, one of many in a world where all social relationships could be ranked along a scale of direct physical marking and control. Instead, the body had become the reflection of racial, cultural, moral, and other abstract differences, all of them entitling different bodies differently. However, because the body stayed, given the physical nature of production and monetary power until the rise of high capitalism, inseparable from the creation of wealth, it still had to be marked as the site of identification/identity. Sublimation and naturalization of differences went hand-in-hand for Nazism to have its effect—and derive its benefits from xenophobic inequalities of power: 'A second subsidiary purpose of the concentration camps, more mundane in character, was the collection and exploitation of SS labour slaves.'[39] Hence, to conclude, one can say that at the core of the Nazi worldview seems to lie the old notion—which we have examined through its tribal, feudal, and early colonial/capitalist manifestations—of the distinctive body of physical belonging. If tribal tattoos or initiation rites were used to mark this body in the remote past, then more abstract notions were employed to define the 'national' (or volk), without changing the fact that the national was born from the body of another national. As historians have pointed out, this, however, was itself a recent construct in some ways, all nations being amalgamations of diverse peoples in the past. But it sufficed. However, determined as it was by capitalism and its ideologies, such as Social Darwinism, the body of belonging in Nazism is also different from the body of the ancient tribal; it exists as a kind of ideal, race or volk or 'ethnicity', which overrides the specific and individual bodies of the *type*. What matters is the 'blood' or 'germ-plasm' or some similarly *abstract* equivalent; it is this that needs to be preserved and spread; the specific individual can be merrily sacrificed to the cause. Hence, bodily identification, while necessary, is made subservient to an abstraction, in keeping with the ways in which money-as-capital operates.

The Body of Old Xenophobia

We have seen how the stranger is defined by old xenophobia as the embodiment of a dangerous difference, a thing out of place like 'dirt', a monster with physical characteristics that are identifiable—and in this the stranger or the out-group (a bunch of largely stereotyped strangers) presents a simplified and distorted aspect of the other to the self, as well as a recognition of the difference that is, by definition, essential to the relationship of the self and the other. Old xenophobia is based on theories of physical and material difference, which is in keeping with the way power operates in a society with limited or no money. As Adam Smith has noted, '[l]abor was the first price, the original purchase-money that was paid for all things. It was not by gold or by silver, but by labor, that all wealth of the world was originally purchased.'[40] Labour, in other words, the human body, with all its physical and material aspects, is not something that could be avoided in the early and even the classical (production-based) phases of capitalism.

But with the rise of highly monetized cultures and, especially, capital, the nature and application of power both become progressively abstract, impacting on the construction and reception of strangers. Old xenophobia, I have argued, *naturalizes* itself with an assumption of physical difference, *borrowed* from earlier times, even when, under the impact of capitalism, these differences increasingly assume abstract underpinnings in the nineteenth century, as mediated by ideologies such as racism, Nazism, and, more complicatedly, nationalisms. Hence, the *naturalization* of tribal, ethnic, physical, biological, genetic, and even linguistic difference, is an essential device of old xenophobia.

The iconic event of old xenophobia, inscribed in our memories and sometimes recurring even today, is genocide, by which a physically segregated population of strangers (often created in the recent past, as is the case with nationalist upheavals) is physically eliminated with the help of physical violence. O'Neill and Hinton note that in the course of the twentieth century alone, 65,000 Hereros, 1 million Armenians, 6 million Ukrainians, 6 million Jews, 3 million Bangladeshis, 1 million Indonesians, 100,000 Hutus, 2 million Cambodians, 200,000 East Timorese, 200,000 Guatemalans, 800,000 Tutsis and moderate Hutus, and millions of indigenous peoples have been annihilated, and 'this is a partial list'.[41] This kind of bodily elimination with the help of physical violence connects old xenophobia to a longer and even older history of xenophobia, but it is a mistake to conflate the two.

Old xenophobia is *not* the xenophobia of pre-monetary societies; it is the xenophobia of monetized societies where labour—and hence the physical and material moorings of the power of money and even capital—cannot be largely evaded. One can return to the common definition of xenophobia as 'a groundless or unreasonable fear of foreigners or strangers or of that which is strange' and refine it further now: xenophobia entails the construction of a stranger or a strangeness to be detested or feared in ways that enable or sustain an institutionally uneven power relation between the self and the other, the in-group and the out-group. Power, as Levinas often suggests, can either bring one face to face with one's responsibility to the other or be used to efface the other. If one recognizes power as being at the core of xenophobia, rather than strangers, fear, difference, etc., then one can see the direct thread that links the so-called milder forms of xenophobia to genocide, which is the ultimate exercise in power over the stranger, as well as conceptualize changes in the nature and scope of xenophobia in keeping with alterations in the way power operates in society.

This notion of the ideal body of belonging makes it easier, perhaps, to identify and persecute the strange/foreign body of difference in many ways, in the simple sense in which the reality always differs from any ideal. While one can choose to overlook the fact that Hitler was neither blond nor tall because he had already inserted himself into 'Aryan' definitions of belonging, it would be always possible to find a sign or a reason or two (as contravening the 'ideal') to exclude a Jew or a Gypsy even if he were tall and blond. The 'body' of the stranger remains 'distinctive' in this way of thinking, which is one that I identify as belonging to old xenophobia. This helps us explain the distinctive marks of difference that characterized Nazism: their need to mark and tag enemies and aliens like Jews and Gypsies. One finds similar tendencies in other European contexts too, as well as among Muslims in the Middle East and among Hindus in India (for instance, in some versions of the caste system).

In old xenophobia, a focus on physical difference—the hooked noses of Jews and Turks, the colour of 'Blacks', the curry smell or effeminate gestures of East Indians, the private parts of women, etc.—was essential as a trigger to fear. Nussbaum shows that the fear of a hidden threat also builds upon this perceived physical difference. She illustrates the similarities between foundational 'modern' anti-Semitic documents, such as the 'Rabbi's Speech' (1872) and the *Protocols of the Elders of Zion* (c. 1902), and much of paranoid anti-Muslim discourse today, such as the 1,500-page 'manifesto' of Anders Behring Breivik, the Norwegian zealot who murdered approximately 76 people in two attacks in Norway in July 2011. All such documents are conspiracy fictions that convey the basic idea that a minority (and beleaguered) group is plotting to achieve world domination and will do so, unless the majority wakes up and takes decisive action. While such texts build on some real problem—economic insecurity, class tensions, political uncertainty, etc.—they serve to displace the fear on to something that has little or nothing to do with the underlying problem and (in the instances quoted above) do so by nourishing the notion of a disguised enemy.

This enemy appears to be the same as us (or pretends and claims to be so), but is secretly plotting for dominance. This connects to the notion of the 'physically' different other that I have noted, but in a subtle way. As Nussbaum notes, 'Group A fantasizes that Group B is oozy, slimy, disgusting, hyper-animal. But the members of Group B look, in fact, like the members of Group A. What could explain this dissonance? They must be hiding something.'[42] This is obviously an element of xenophobia even today, though I consider it an aspect of old xenophobia. 'Old', in this usage, does not mean 'over'. Cultural practices have a life that resists material changes, and in any case many lives and societies in the world are still partly structured by the kind of socio-economic realities that framed what I have termed old xenophobia.

4

CAPITAL AND NEW XENOPHOBIA

Today, the most visible issues that concern minorities (Muslims, for instance) in many 'developed' countries, especially in social welfare states like Switzerland, Denmark, and Holland, run *against* the logic of old xenophobia documented in the previous chapter. Old xenophobia, as I have illustrated, insisted on the visibility of the stranger; Jews were not just supposed to be visible, they were perforce made visible by the state (and not just the Nazi state). When they ceased to be visible, their presence led to intricate theories of conspiracy: they were just hiding their difference, waiting for a chance to emerge in their true colours and reveal their true nature. An aspect of this exists in the current anti-Muslim discourse too, but then old xenophobia has cultural and actual forms that do not evaporate entirely. What is far more interesting is that the real controversies today, put to extremely xenophobic uses at times, relate to the burqa and to the minaret. There is a problem here: the burqa and minarets make strangers *more* visible. In this sense, they are the equivalent of the visible tagging that old xenophobia preferred to inflict on strangers. But in this case, they *are* the problem. If violence was done to Jews and others by old xenophobia to *mark* them as strangers, violence is now being done to some religious Muslims and immigrants in order *to prevent them from standing out*, visibly, as strangers. Why?

'You safe?' I texted a (white) friend in London when images of the city burning flashed on television screens during the England riots of August 2011. 'No fear,' she texted back. 'Our locality is protected by Turks.'

What's happening in London, television commentators kept asking in Denmark, where I am based. Experts who pointed to growing social inequalities, and to the fact that working-class people (many of them, inevitably, from recent immigrant backgrounds) feel discriminated against at times, were often prodded to give explanations in terms of 'culture' or even 'religion', but *never* colour or race.

Interestingly, just two days earlier, I had read in a leading Danish newspaper that every tenth Dane was arming himself against home robberies. This was in keeping with the trend of a high percentage of interviewed Danes often claiming to be afraid of burglaries. Denmark was not burning; so, what was wrong here? Had there been a spate of home burglaries in Denmark?

According to state police figures, only 359 home robberies were registered all over Denmark in 2009, and the 2011 figure is estimated to be around the same. This means that less than 0.015 per cent of Danish homes were robbed in 2009. Actually, in 2010, Denmark saw a drop in burglaries of private residences reported to the police for the first time in three years. According to police statistics, burglaries dropped by approximately 6 per cent between 2009 and 2010.

In other words, the numbers did not explain why every tenth Dane was arming himself against home burglaries. Denmark appeared to be suffering from a heightened state of paranoia. So did other advanced countries, if media reports are an indication. The shooting and bombing spree of the Christian fundamentalist and Far Right nationalist Anders Behring Breivik in Norway on 22 July 2011, was partly an extreme expression of that paranoia. The fact that ordinary Danes find themselves threatened in their own homes and are willing to arm themselves against a 0.01 per cent possibility of a home robbery is another expression of this paranoia. There are many other versions of this fear.

Breivik, whom we have met before, is a good starting point for our discussion. In the case of both the London riots and Breivik's murderous actions, we encounter exceptions—the very obvious violence of the two 'events' is a case to point—that, nevertheless, help us understand what might be going on. I first heard of the Norway attacks some hours after they had taken place, on my way to the Hong Kong book fair on 22 July. TV screens in Copenhagen and Helsinki, where I had to change flights, reported the tragedy. The details were unclear then; I was rushing to catch my flights. Oh no, I recall thinking, another crazy Islamist! I shuddered at the thought of the deaths and suffering, as well as the usual rhetoric against immigrants, Muslims, and multiculturalism that I could imagine being spouted in many European quarters.

On my return to Denmark, I was told by Danish friends that some Danish newspapers had already jumped the gun—and blamed the atrocities on Islamists and Al-Qaeda. Here, it needs to be noted, that there is a difference between such hasty media accounts and the suspicion that had crossed my mind—or that might cross the minds of Hr and Fru Hansen. Hr and Fru Hansen, like me, do not publish their opinions and hence do not add to the prejudices and the jargon of certain political parties; media accounts are not meant to be hasty, nor are they supposed to be based on cultural stereotypes. Ask yourself: what if the perpetrator of the crimes had never been discovered? What if no one had ever discovered his real identity? Who would have borne the blame then, and which kinds of parties would have reaped the benefits of this tragedy?

By the time I reached Hong Kong on 23 July, the details were clearer. There had been a car bomb explosion outside the executive government offices of Oslo in the afternoon, killing and critically wounding about 20 people. The second attack had occurred less than two hours later at a camp organized by the youth wing of the Norwegian Labour Party (AP) on the peaceful island of Utøya. A gunman, disguised as a policeman, had cold-bloodedly opened sustained fire at the participants, killing about 70 attendees, including personal friends of Prime Minister Jens Stoltenberg and a stepbrother of Norway's crown princess. The Norwegian police soon arrested Breivik, a 32-year-old man, and charged him with both attacks.

Relief is not the right word to describe the emotions experienced in the wake of such a senseless tragedy, and yet, coming from where I did, I felt something like relief on learning that Breivik was a light-haired, light-eyed, white Norwegian nationalist who apparently considered himself a 'Christian' and had Rightist sympathies. As such, I was a bit surprised when fingers continued to be pointed accusingly at immigrants and at multiculturalism in the West.

Some discussion of 'multiculturalism' and immigration, which Breivik claimed to be fighting, was necessary. Such discussions reminded me of intellectuals, including Muslim ones, who try to understand the causes of Islamist terror. And yet, there were European voices that seemed less than honest, just as there are Muslims who sound less than honest when faced with Islamist atrocities. Writers and intellectuals from places as different as Denmark and France suggested that the real culprit was not Breivik, but 'multiculturalism'.

Of course! Multiculturalism has moved from being the panacea of the lazy politician to becoming the Devil for virulent leaders all across Europe today. I, like some other scholars from postcolonial societies, never liked the first version of multiculturalism, as it appeared to be largely the result of political convenience and economic expediency. In the booming post-war decades when Europe needed cheap labour for reconstruction, multiculturalism was purloined from academia and repeated as a mantra by lazy politicians. It could be used to justify and manipulate the entry of cheap non-European labour as well as to make overspending European middle classes feel good about their excursions into ethnic garments, exotic travel, foreign cuisine, etc. More, it seldom was, even in England and France, where it was a weightier factor than in the narrower and heavily regulated societies of North Europe despite their (at that time) official discourses. Now, with the boom over and unemployment figures rising, suddenly politicians, from England to Germany and Holland, have discovered that multiculturalism does not work.

The problem is not just that multiculturalism could not work, for it was never formulated with an honest desire to confront problems and to explain advantages without eulogizing or demonizing other peoples. In this sense, xenophobia and (some kinds of) xenophilia end up fuelling one another, and are equally blind to the lived reality of the other. The problem with the boomerang effect of a dismissal of multiculturalism by leading European politicians today is that it feeds into rightist and racist assumptions about the supposed purity of national cultures or 'Europe'. Such myths are historically as untrue as the Islamist myth of religious purity and of an Islamic golden age. It is such lopsided legends, not multiculturalism, that create a Breivik. Multiculturalism, however defective, was a necessary antidote to such logically genocidal constructs of purity. Glibly blaming multiculturalism is as dishonest as it was once to let Hitler blame Jews and Gypsies. This aspect of the attack on multiculturalism—as well as the predominant 'official' positions on multiculturalism as a material sharing of the pie of governmental patronage—places it partly under the rubric of old xenophobia. But, just as interestingly, multiculturalism also has a different function in new xenophobia. It is a thoroughly abstract monster, unlike Jews, Gypsies, and coloured immigrants, whose monstrosity was always physical (and remains so) in the eyes of old xenophobia. That this abstract monster often encompasses old categories of physical monsters, is both significant and beside the point in this context.

Europe's problem of subterranean xenophobia is different from that of the USA; it is less individual and more structural. One can (as I often do) admire the social welfare systems that distinguish many rich European nations from the rich USA, and yet this difference is at the heart of Europe's burgeoning new xenophobia. Given its colonial advantages of market and wealth, early insertion into industrialization and capitalism, as well as its radical thinkers and movements (trade unions), on the one side, and its progressive conservatives and liberals, on the other, European countries started moving towards social welfare states in the late nineteenth century and mostly achieved them around the mid-twentieth century. This historic European compromise between labour and capital enabled European capital to move more or less freely, but protected European workers, raising them effectively to the status of the middle class in places like Scandinavia.

But it was based on a contradiction because capitalism is, even by liberal definition (as I have highlighted), based on the free movement of both capital and labour. And despite political rhetoric, international labour is far less free to move than global capital. In a globalizing world, European states can protect the 'social welfare' privileges of their citizens only by manipulating the exclusion of non-European workers who try to follow capital in search of better wages. This exclusion, though, involves highly *abstract* forms of exclusion and inclusion. While European wealth accrues from the relatively free movement of capital across borders, European welfare states are seen as being based on the imposition of strong and strict controls on the movement of (non-European) labour. The occlusion of the nature of high capitalism—its power and violence—is essential to this equation.

Ergo, the European Right with its worries about national identity and the European Left with its worries about falling wages! There is very little difference on both sides at times in terms of the actual impact on strangers in these spaces. Both basically do not want workers—except a few who are highly educated and who pay their way in after getting their home countries, like India, to subsidize their higher education—from other 'cultures' in Europe anymore. Unspoken xenophobia is the vampire that stalks the mansion of European social welfare prosperity.

The USA, with its flaws of national inequity, has a more honest structure, partly because of its self-conception, as Nussbaum also notes. With a historical consciousness of migration as the basis of the nation state, the USA (or, for that matter, a social welfare state like Canada) allows a bit more mobility to labour, including international labour. Moreover, given the great economic and social differences in the USA and its acute history of race relations, a large part of the xenophobia in the USA is still old xenophobia, based on ingrained definitions of physical difference, sustained by the faltering production-based mega-machines of classical capitalism that still grind on internally. This explains, for instance, the inability of such American racists to distinguish between Muslims and

Sikhs when they go on a shooting spree. It also explains the difference between such racist shootouts in the USA, aimed at physically eradicating the visibly different, and Breivik's much more abstract selection of victims. Breivik did not target those who looked different; instead, he chose to shoot those who looked like he did himself—ethnically Nordic citizens of Norway—because he felt that they had allowed those who were essentially different (that is, Muslims) into Norway. He was not directly focused on physical differences or similarities; this factor did not make a difference in his selection of victims. His main grouse was far more abstract: 'multiculturalism', which he felt had been allowed to flourish in Norway by left-leaning Norwegians. Moreover, Breivik implicitly defined even his stranger as being different in the abstract *and* in essence; that is, made different by his religiosity and religion, by his political tendencies, etc., all of which this odious stranger was nefariously going to impose on Norway and Europe. While internal or in-group conflicts are known in all societies, the option that Breivik adopted is relatively new. His was not just an in-group conflict or violence aimed at an out-group, which are both common historically. Rather, his violence targeted members of an in-group because of his resentment of an out-group. Unlike the case of many previous types of xenophobia, the out-group was not made a sacrificial scapegoat here, but more of an abstract scapegoat. The actual victims of Breivik's xenophobia were members of the in-group. His hostility to the out-group was no doubt intense, but it remained abstract even in its acting out. One can argue that this added to Breivik's paranoia.

This conscious or unconscious creation of paranoia is at the heart of what I have called new xenophobia. Only some of the paranoia can be attributed to the actual possibility of threats, such as those from Islamist terrorism. Most of it is the creation of a certain kind of political and media discourse. I will not waste space by highlighting once again the increasingly xenophobic tone adopted by politicians from the Far Right, and sometimes even from the traditional Left, in these countries. The suspicion of strangers, the growing intolerance of immigrants, the easy slippage from a gimmicky version of multiculturalism to a gimmicky dismissal of it, the increasing tendency to hector minorities instead of entering into a mutually respectful dialogue with them—these tendencies have been exhibited by a number of politicians, including some mainstream ones, from England to Norway.

Combine these tendencies with the current global economic downslide, which is partly the result of the increasing complicity of politicians with free-floating financial interests, and the fact, obvious to any thinking person today, that corporations and banks can lose millions of other people's money and be bailed out by governments, but the same generosity is seldom extended to ordinary citizens and never to really poor ones. This combination provides one with a better understanding of, say, the London violence than 'religion' or 'culture'. It was old-fashioned material violence, no doubt, and hence it was highly visible to us, but behind it lurked newfangled forms of abstract violence that even intellectuals of the status of Steven Pinker fail to see.

What is even less visible is another sort of mis-reportage that adds, very subtly, to xenophobia and even racist prejudices. A couple of years ago, for instance, widespread reports of the gradual 'disappearance' of the gene for blondness appeared in the media. Many media reports of matters like 'genetic research' are slanted towards simplistic phrenology-type assumptions, and this one was a significant example. It was simply wrong;

neither the scientific survey nor the scientific body behind this purported study of the disappearance of the blonde gene existed. But while British newspapers investigated the report (after publishing it) and later carried rebuttals (less visibly), I do not recall seeing any such correction in the Danish media. Actually, the fact remains that such hoaxes are often slipped in, or fed to the media, not as 'jokes', but because they (consciously or subconsciously) reinforce xenophobic prejudices. New xenophobia prefers to talk of slightly abstracted matters like 'blonde' genes, while old xenophobia would have spoken of the threat to the 'Aryan race' and the nose of the Jew.

The matter is not relegated to media discourse alone; it pervades more intellectual and scientific forms of discourse too. Pichot has highlighted this with reference to the works of E.O. Wilson (*Sociobiology: The New Synthesis*) and Richard Dawkins (*The Selfish Gene*). He has pointed out that in both these influential books, the gene returns to stand in for the 'individual' in the theory of Darwinian selection. Pichot gives a number of extensive illustrations to substantiate the point, but perhaps the title of Dawkins's book (probably left out as being too obvious by Pichot) is itself the best example of the trend and its assumptions: what kind of 'self' does a gene have? And if it does not have a 'self', can the idea of a 'selfish' gene—even as an allegory—be devoid of some deeply personified ideological assumptions about the human individual?

As seen earlier, Pichot has also illustrated that the Darwinian postulates of natural selection and survival of the fittest as the mechanisms of evolution could not be scientifically proved either by Darwin or by his followers, despite becoming orthodoxy by the early twentieth century, largely for ideological reasons. When the mechanism of evolution could be scientifically traced—with the rise of genetics in the twentieth century—it actually worked against the Darwinian postulates of survival of the fittest and natural selection by highlighting the role of mutation and random selection. Following years in the wilderness, however, with books like Dawkins's *The Selfish Gene*, many of these implicit assumptions have donned the highly abstract garb of genes and numerical charts and models.

Pichot convincingly highlights the ways in which both Wilson and, more crudely, Dawkins personify genes, so that genes seem to operate like individuals. Pichot traces the 'genetic mysticism' of early twentieth-century ideologues of eugenics, such as Vacher de Lapouge and his pseudo-scientific notion of the 'germplasm', in highly abstract form, to the 'Dawkinian' notion of genes basically perpetuating and multiplying more of their 'own' kind. Dawkins uses pseudo-scientific notions, such as that of 'kin-altruism', to explain how and why the selfish gene prefers its own 'kin'. Obviously, while Dawkins does not face up to the problem, we are very close here to older notions of blood, race, and heredity. These might or might not be what Dawkins intends, but they can be readily inferred from his book and from similar popular studies of genetics. The kind of expert knowledge of genes that would prevent such faulty inferences only exists at the highest levels of study and research, among scientists specializing in the field, and even there, given the fragmentation induced by necessary specialization, probably not among all scientists. This has enabled the return of such matters as 'blonde genes' and 'genes for crime' in media discourse. At a highly abstract level—for genes are in their very conceptualization highly abstract, regardless of what they might be in actual existence—this has managed to both preserve and obscure the old xenophobic physicalities of race, colour, etc. For instance, it is common, as media reports indicate, for mainstream politicians to indulge in old-fashioned anti-Gypsy prejudices with reference to new-fashioned 'genetic' discourses on criminality.[1]

There is an additional consequence of such a development: the growing abstraction of social, political, and scientific 'facts' twisted together in such a way as to create a state of siege in the minds of many Europeans. I do not claim that all such concoctions are deliberate. Most of them simply reflect the unexamined prejudices of their writers, more so in cultures, like Norway, Holland, or Denmark, where people see themselves as basically open and hence unprejudiced by definition. Such reports are substantiated by a spate of invasion and action films—where 'humans' are invaded by apes, insects, UFOS, etc., and the only real option is complete destruction on the one or the other side. Breivik's 'reality' shared elements of this fantasy. The Swedish historian, Sven Lindqvist, has documented in "Exterminate All the Brutes" that 'invasion scare' stories were particularly popular in the first half of the twentieth century—the decades that saw the rise of fascism. Now, I suspect, they are back in more abstract forms. It is creating vast provinces of paranoia.

But all this is not new. Old xenophobia contained aspects or versions of similar constructions of the self and the other. The question remains: why, today, the desire to arm yourself when only 0.01 per cent of your homes get burgled? Why the need to demonize immigrants when you know and see that the vast majority are law-abiding citizens? Why the longing to see Europe as a 'pure' space (not of physical race now but of abstract values, like democracy) when a spate of studies, such as Jonathan Lyons's *The House of Wisdom* and Ian Almond's *Two Faiths, One Banner*, indicate how much Europe has shared with other cultures (including Arab ones) all through history? Why the recent choice of culture/religion over colour, race, and even class as explanation in societies where social inequalities are steadily increasing? Why the return of Social Darwinist ideas (or similar ones) in the more abstract garb of popular genetics, when actually scientific genetics has long disproved them?

The history of European old xenophobia is not sufficient as explanation. What is happening has more to do with the present than with the past. Rich nations in Europe are increasingly behaving like rich people in places like India, South Africa, and the Caribbean do, and for largely the same reasons. They are erecting electrified fences around their residential colonies.

European welfare states—which managed, partly by their own endeavours and partly by the favours of colonial history and capitalist dominance in the world, to raise their own poor citizens out of desperate poverty—are particularly paranoid. These admirable welfare states are not sufficient. Their welfare privileges finally depend on their dominance in a world of capitalism—their AAA and AA+ ratings—that can only be maintained if their capital can flow around and freely exploit the wealth and the labour of the entire globe. But along with this, there arises a problem: that of labour following capital to seek better wages, and capital following cheap labour in search of higher profits. Both processes/phenomena are inevitable. But both will also inevitably affect European welfare privileges.

The European middle classes want the benefits of capitalism, but they do not always want to pay the price. With historical logic finally catching up with them, they do not even want to face this contradiction. Paranoia—the word I used instead of fear in this chapter—involves a kind of abstract and faceless fear. In this sense too, the fear cultivated by new xenophobia differs from that propagated by old xenophobia. Though certain strangers are made the face of this paranoia, what lurks behind them is the vast, faceless machine of high capitalism, those abstract and numerical flows of capital that impinge on our lives without becoming visible. To address this abstract source of paranoia would require not just a paradigm shift, but also a change in lifestyles and priorities. It is easier to find a focus for this source of anxiety, leading to paranoia, in the increasingly abstract construction of the stranger of new xenophobia, for this stranger is not just scapegoat, but actually also a highly distorted *proof* of that vast invisible machine of numbers that grinds on and on and is never fully comprehended or addressed. This stranger is constructed in increasingly abstract terms also because its source is anxiety and paranoia, not just fear.

Hence, the choice of culture (increasingly seen as 'religion' too), rather than the Leftist 'class' or even the old Rightist 'race', as an explanation offered by new xenophobia. Inevitably, this new mutation of xenophobia is likely to be the unstated religion of the European middle classes, safe inside their electrified fences, regardless of whether they vote Left or Right. In this, they are aided by the non-European Right, such as Islamists, with their own versions of old xenophobia.

Here we return, past the gates of social welfare states and 'enlightened democracies', to a spectre that has recently started haunting the world ... or maybe, more accurately in a discursive sense, the globe. Like all spectres, it seems to have risen from the dead. The spectre is religion. Half a century ago, religion was supposed to be well past its sell-by date, in intellectual terms. Today, it is very much a matter of contention. Islam, in particular, is the religion most of us have in mind, but it is not the only one. Other religions have been used to create and persecute strangers in ways that, half a century ago, some thought were safely consigned to the Middle Ages. And in some ways, they were right. The recent return of religions is a matter very different from whatever took place during the Crusades. For one, the current notoriety of Islam as *the* problematic religion is not surprising; Islam is the only other major world religion, apart from Christianity (which in its Protestant 'cultural' versions is deeply immersed in capitalism and 'secular' nation-state patronage) which has been adamantly universalist from its inception. Interestingly, even religions— such as Judaism and Hinduism—that were not universalist (one had to be born a Hindu or a Jew; until recently one could not convert) have taken over universalist contours in recent decades.

This, in itself, indicates a change. Evidently, religions, in more or less universalist versions, are back in the fray under the globalism of high capitalism. More than that, they have been divided into the good guys and the bad guys. The good guys are religions or the religious that fade into the high capitalist culture of today. Protestant versions—undergirded by consumerism, secularized rituals, and state churches (in most European countries)—obviously enjoy an advantage here, but basically this club is open to others too. The bad guys are those who insist on 'old-fashioned' rituals, traditions, laws, clothing, etc. They insist on obviously material/physical structures of power: Islamist versions of Islam, for instance, but also, largely, orthodox Hindus, or orthodox Jews, or orthodox Roman Catholics. This development casts an illuminating light on our discussion of old and new xenophobia.

Martha C. Nussbaum's *The New Religious Intolerance* is an insightful and pertinent study of xenophobia along the lines of this revival of religions. She starts off by noting that once, 'not very long ago, Americans and Europeans prided themselves on their enlightened attitudes of religious tolerance and understanding', and thought that 'religious violence was somewhere else—in societies more "primitive," less characterized by a heritage of Christian values than were the modern social democracies of Europe'. Putting on record the common fact that both Europe and the United States, but much more so the former, have a history of religious intolerance, she notes that Europe is particularly conditioned by a stress on homogeneity, often in terms of a recently constructed nation-statism that blurs culture, nation, and religion in subtle ways. She remarks that countries like India, the USA, and Australia have their own kinds of intolerance, but are at least saved by their national self-constructions from insisting on a natural homogeneity that automatically secludes strangers. Nussbaum points out that even in the context of the post-war self-perception of Europeans and Americans as tolerant, recent events have given us 'many reasons to doubt this complacent self-assessment'. She goes on to convincingly list many of these events and pieces of evidence directed against visible foreigners and Muslims. Fear is accelerating, she notes.[2]

Nussbaum argues that while fear had its evolutionary advantages and continues to have positive political uses today, it is nevertheless a very basic emotion, one that we share with other animals and birds: fear has to do with primitive brain processes shared by all vertebrates, and its animal origin delimits the extent of its narcissistic comprehension of reality. Nussbaum hastens to add that the shared animal origins of 'fear' is no reason to dismiss it: fear can be accurate, but its view of the world is extremely limited; unlike sympathy or grief, Nussbaum notes, fear does not concede the equivalent reality of other people.[3] Moreover, human fear is in at least one way much worse than animal fear, for animals do not construct themselves as pure and non-animalistic while fantasizing about other groups of animals as foul and dirty. '[H]uman fear combines animal narrowness with a peculiarly human shrinking from animality—in other groups of people, where animality is always imagined.'[4]

Nussbaum shows that old xenophobic texts build on some real problem—economic insecurity, class tensions, political uncertainty, etc.—but they serve to displace the fear on to something that has little or nothing to do with the underlying problem, and that they often do so by engendering the idea of a disguised enemy. This enemy appears to be the 'same as us', or pretends and claims to be so, but is secretly plotting for dominance. This connects to the notion of the 'physically' different other that I have noted, but in a subtle way.

This insistence on 'hiding' something is further complicated in the current revival of religions: take, for instance, the 'Muslim' case of the over-all burqa. Nussbaum points out, convincingly, that while the burqa can be criticized (in my view, it should be criticized), it is a minor observance among Muslims (many of whom do not wear the burqa) and all the European reasons for banning it are either faulty or open to criticism in terms of consequentiality, even-handedness, etc. However, this is an argument I do not want to enter. The only reason I have brought up the burqa is that it provides a very interesting way of conceptualizing the differences between what I term old xenophobia and new xenophobia, and enables us to understand the 'return of religion'.

In terms of old xenophobia, as outlined above, the burqa could not really symbolize an innocent covering ('disguise') under which an enemy—the different other—lurked. The burqa, as a visibly different mode of dress, made the enemy visible. This was not bad in the eyes of old xenophobia. Old xenophobia preferred to have the stranger marked by a visible indication of difference. For old xenophobia, the burqa would have been somewhat similar to the Star of David.

But today there is a double (or triple) bind to the burqa. First, the woman under the burqa is usually a coloured immigrant and hence, in the racist physical terms of old xenophobia, a visible stranger. Second, the burqa does not disguise her non-disguisable difference (in physical old xenophobic terms). Third, as she dons a burqa in a society where the vast majority does not wear it, the burqa actually serves as an anti-disguise; it makes her *more* visible. So, in this case, we do not have someone who looks like 'us' and we do not have a disguise that makes this different other pass for us. In many scenarios of old societies, it would have been fully permissible to don a burqa; actually, one can even imagine some European societies insisting on this outward sign of difference for Muslim women, just as they had insisted on outward signs of difference for Jews in the past. This, however, is not the case with the burqa. In order to understand this, we need to return to Nussbaum's analysis of fear, and then insert it into the current historical context.

This is what Nussbaum says about the limits of fear as a guide to our reactions to others today, despite its evolutionary and current usefulness in many contexts:

Human societies are still threatened by many natural forces and diseases [as in our evolutionary past, which made 'fear' such a useful emotion], but they are also threatened by human hostility, by war, poverty, and dangers yet more abstract than these (economic catastrophe, group discrimination, lack of political and religious liberty, social revolution) [...]. This means that human beings have to make decisions in a world for which evolution has given them only very rudimentary preparation. If fear is to be a helpful motivator in that world, then people have to form a conception of their own safety and well-being, and that of their society, that is considerably more complicated than the narrow evolutionary focus on short-term bodily safety, and they have to engage in sophisticated thinking about what threatens that well-being.[5]

This analysis of the role and limits of fear fits our understanding of old xenophobia; it requires an intellectual and emotional effort on our part to understand that body-based fear, which is perhaps reflected in the physical signs by which old xenophobia mostly operated, is not sufficient for our well-being. Once we overcome this evolutionary limitation, we have set ourselves on the road to tackling our real problems.

I argue in this book that no matter how valid this understanding is to any bid to overcome old xenophobia, it falls short of the structures of new xenophobia. That is so because new xenophobia is not based solely on our evolutionary fear for our bodily safety; it is also based in many societies (especially socio-economically developed ones) on those societies' non-body-centred and complex 'conception of their own safety and well-being' and on their ability to 'engage in sophisticated thinking about what threatens that well-being'. It does not depend on a body-centred narcissism, but on certain understandings of social cohesion and even, with some nuances, care for others in that society.

At its base lies the main economic development of high capitalism or globalization that is often overlooked or not explored today: the relationship between welfare, capital, and labour at the national and international levels. From this perspective, if we go back to the burqa, we can see something a bit more complex: the burqa is not a disguise under which the different other lurks. The other, inside the burqa, is already physically different, and, moreover, the burqa does not hide this difference; if anything, it makes it even more obvious, glaringly so. However, what the burqa does that is disturbing, and all European opposition to it fits into this category of understanding, is that it imposes a different symbolic order on the already different body of the woman underneath. This woman—who, without the burqa, is simply that problematic but definable construct 'immigrant labour', which has been abstracted by capital—turns into a living symbol of a different structure of power, and one that cannot be fully circumscribed by abstract capital. The burqa does not hide the immigrant labourer (and it does not matter if the woman works or not); it cannot. What it does do is shake the empowering and *abstract* structures of identity imposed by *abstract* global capital, partly by making the immigrant labourer not just more visible, but also opaque to the logic of capitalism, where proper bodies exist only at the cost of the increasingly invisible labouring body.

What is truly disturbing about the woman in a burqa under new xenophobia is the return of the body as a difference. This sometimes translates into concern for the woman, as a female body oppressed by Islamist patriarchy. But finally as some legislative recommendations suggest—in the sense that they offer an extreme choice to the woman to either work or wear a burqa, instead of ensuring that she would, as woman and worker, be assured of the basic right to work first of all— the attempt is to make the body of this difference invisible. One can make a similar argument with reference to other core issues of new xenophobia, such as objections to the building of a minaret in various European countries.

It is in this context that religion becomes useful on all sides. If we confine ourselves to the main ('Islam versus Europe') conflict, we see that Islamists use religion to suggest the physical enactment of an identity that is essential to their worldview, and would have been compulsory in the past in Europe too (and might be essential even today in European circles less absorbed into the ambit/orbit of high capitalism), while liberals and neo-liberals react to this counter-construction, which is felt as a threat to the invisible universality of capital. The great irony of this double movement is that the consumerism of capitalism allows, and even enforces, the purchase of various kinds of 'differences', so that under new xenophobia, for instance, a hundred different dresses bought on a single day is not a problem, but a burqa is; varieties of piercings are tolerated, but circumcision is problematic. In each case, the mind of high capitalist citizens of rich countries is distinguishing between the power of capital, which can be allowed to impinge on the body, and some other avenue of power that can also have an impact on the body. In the process, a new stranger is created. This is the stranger whose body is visibly constructed by networks of power other than those of high capitalism. Once again, religion returns as a candidate in two broad ways. The monster is back, but this is a monster whose very physicality is the problem, and it is a problem because it threatens the monopoly of power exercised by or demanded by high capital. This monster can only stop being seen as a threat by new xenophobia if it abstracts itself totally into the identical networks of high capitalism.

In one way, religion becomes shorthand for the essential difference of this new stranger. Religion is not race or colour; it can have any race or colour (though, and this explains the overlap between old racists and new xenophobia at times, it can contain more of one colour or 'race' than another). Axial-age religions might also offer, as Duchrow and Hinkelammert argue, a genuine site of opposition to the power of capital, in their suspicion of money and opposition to interest. This, though, should not be turned into a revolutionary celebration of religious subversion because, as I have argued throughout this book, opposition to the structures of power of capital (or even money) presupposes other (physical and material) structures of power.

Abstractions of New Xenophobia

Morey and Yaqin begin by listing some by-now-typical post-9/11 headlines on Muslims: 'Islam and Freedom: Are They Destined to Clash?' (*Newsweek*); 'Muhammad Cartoon Row Intensifies' (BBC); 'Burka Makes Women Prisoners, Says President Sarkozy' (*Times*); 'Universities Urged to Spy on Muslims' (*The Guardian*). They then go on to note that such reportage and commentary seem 'unanimous in the picture they paint of Muslims: unenlightened outsiders who, while they may live and work in the West, still have an allegiance to values different from those recognized in Europe and North America'. They add that '[s]uch images are distorted abstractions. Extrapolating from context-specific controversies, they paint Muslims as a homogenous, zombie-like body, incapable of independent thought and liable to be whipped into frenzy at the least disturbance to their unchanging backward worldview.'⁶ A veritable cottage industry of minor literature and films, such as *Ozombie* (in which Osama bin Laden returns as a zombie, replete with hoards of zombie Islamic terrorists) is growing out of this worldview in the West and, despite make-belief and irony, these fictions reinforce factual belief in 'distorted abstractions' about the Muslim-stranger.

'Distorted abstractions' are at the core of xenophobia, old or new; or, more exactly, 'abstractions' are, for abstractions always entail distortion of some sort. However, as I have argued in this book, old xenophobia has in mind a physical and material difference that paralleled the largely physical and material (money- or trade-based) nature of early and production-based capitalism. With the greater abstraction of capital, the monsters of this xenophobic physicality become progressively abstract; abstract elements are attributed to their monstrosity by nationalism, which abstracts on the basis of ethnicity and/or linguistic 'purity'; or even by racism, as an abstract and institutionalized system of racial differences. These elements retain a physical or material base, so to say: racism, anti-Semitism, etc., gestured at moral, ethical, and other differences, but remained rooted in implicit or explicit definitions of physical and material prototypes. However, with the rise of high capitalism, we have a move to a completely different notion of abstract power—capital as numbers, and not money as medium or social relation. This restructures the understanding of xenophobia in 'advanced' sections of high capitalist societies, mostly, but not only, in the First World. In keeping with prior construction of identities (usually via old xenophobia) and, in many rich countries, the unfaced contradiction of labour/capital in social welfare states, new xenophobia turns its gaze on bodies that, in their physicality, are not fully or largely enabled (and hence made invisible/inoffensive) by high capital. It focuses on not all immigrants, but 'illegal' immigrants; not all Muslims, but 'religious' Muslims; etc.

One can argue, following Charles Taylor, that old and new xenophobia build, in different ways, on the modern buffered self's capacity and need for abstractions. The common reactionary attempt to circumnavigate the unreality or hyperreality of such abstractions is always based on an attempt to turn the clock back to an actual encounter with a particular type of stranger. Hence, the newspapers continue to suggest, for instance, that Gypsies or Muslim immigrants are inclined towards criminality. This is also done by commenting on an actual case, for example, of theft or rape, in which the ethnicity, religion, non-native origin, etc., of the suspect or criminal is highlighted, that is, when this suspect or criminal belongs to one such minority group. In effect, such reportage, consciously or not, tries to provide a particular and grounded rationale for xenophobia.

The deeply faulty, but often emotionally effective, logic of this works as follows: it is natural to be frightened of a stranger who breaks into my apartment with the intention to rob. There is this stranger who barged into XYZ's apartment and robbed it. This stranger was an immigrant, as the tabloids highlighted (while forgetting to note in the case of a dozen other break-ins that the burglar was *not* an immigrant). Hence, it is natural to be wary of strangers like immigrants. QED.

Of course, while the first line is a valid statement, all the others are spurious inferences, based on the capacity of the thinker to turn one specific case into an abstract type. The fear of a stranger encountered in your apartment is not the same as the fear of strangers per se. The former is a specific incident; the latter is based on abstraction: the one stranger is conflated with all other abstract strangers (people seen as sharing a particularly abstract quality of strangeness, however defined) who are then to be feared or disliked generically and outside any specific context. In high capitalism, the stranger who enters wearing the garb of capital–power is largely tolerated, even welcomed at the highest governmental and business levels, but the stranger who dons the burqa of other structures of power is strongly opposed, not as a physical monstrosity, but as an abstract 'physical' monstrosity. What makes this stranger a monster is no longer his physical/material differences, but the abstract or essence of another empowering structure of identity that constitutes his *body* as out of place in a world of freely circulating high capital.

It needs to be added that capital, which is largely universal, is not—and perhaps, by its very nature, cannot be—totally self-sufficient. As capital at its purest and most abstract is finally nothing but numbers, some of its value or power will depend on older forms of material value or power: coin, gold, mineral wealth, food product, human product, etc. Hence, it is impossible to break the link between money and capital (regardless of what idealists or communists might claim), though, of course, only someone who is unaware of how the global world of finance operates will confuse the two. Similarly, it is impossible to break the link between money and products or precious items—the objects that money mediated or mediates in terms of value—but there are probably no societies left in the world today that cannot distinguish between the two conceptual categories. Hence, various other avenues of value and power operate by the side of capital, though it is capital that is globally dominant today.

Some types of power have always been, and will remain, physical and material, given the nature of human beings. As human beings are always embodied materially and physically in life, their bodies can be empowered or punished materially and physically. A human body can always be bullied, whipped, imprisoned, and executed, and these options are not going to disappear as long as human bodies remain conditional to human existence. One can even argue that at a certain level, capital accumulation needs to depend on the possibility of these 'prior' kinds of physical and material violence. In a 'globalizing' world, this helps us understand not just 9/11, but also why the USA and its allies had to strike back *physically* at the culprits—real, imagined, or concocted—of the heinous crime of 9/11. Hence, of course, the police and the army, among other control appendages. Hence, the tendency in some rich capitalist nations to imprison and execute. The point is not that such manifestations of power have disappeared, or will disappear, but rather that they will be mediated through capital. This will happen (in 'civilized' countries) in two major ways: capital will be used as the primary mode of control and empowerment (fines, salaries, taxes, etc.), and physical and material power will be controlled by the nation state, whose source of real power (finance capital) is no longer substantially within state control.

Today, no understanding of violence can work if it leaves out the manifestations of violence through capital, and through the heavily capitalized nation state which needs to facilitate free-floating finance capital simply in order to survive on the currently definitive terms of high capitalism. If our understanding of violence confines itself to physical violence, such a definition implicitly puts the blame of violence only on the 'other side'; that is, those who do not have capital or enough capital to exert power primarily through capital. Hence, if a corporation fires 50 employees, it is not violence. But if the employees protest by blocking the road or perhaps even by throwing stones at the office of the corporate head, it is violence.

But obviously, before we can do violence to others, we have to construct them as dangerous others, as hostile or devious strangers. Old xenophobia could largely do so with reference to physical and material differences, in terms of colour, clothing, skull shape, whatever. Even when more abstract religions came into the mix, they were structured by largely visible signs of difference; not just the Star of David, but the proverbial hooked noses of Jews were absolutely necessary for anti-Semitism in the past. Many of these signs were sustained by appeals to ethnic and tribal myths, while already being more abstract than such appeals suggested. But whatever the difference, a stranger always had to be constructed in terms of identifiable differences—before he could be tolerated or eradicated. Today, in some highly privileged circles and among those influenced by them, a new stranger is being created. As always, he tells us more about ourselves.

This is the stranger whose body is not 'free' (to be inscribed by capital). Incidentally, it goes almost unremarked that such strangers are also workers who cannot travel the 'free markets of globalization' with anything near the mobility enjoyed by capital. This is also the stranger who, as he has not much apart from his constrained body, indulges in acts of physical violence. As we have seen in the case of that paradigmatic threatening stranger, the vampire, this excess on his part calls for his surveillance, eradication, or banishment. In short, we can only explore the nature of the violence of new xenophobia if we look at what violence meant, and what it still means. A recent book by Steven Pinker makes this, quite inadvertently, easier for me to trace.

5

DECEPTIVE VIOLENCE

Steven Pinker's book *The Better Angels of Our Nature* claims that violence has declined since pre-historical times. Pinker questions the ideological assumption that we are living in *increasingly* violent times. He correctly notes that by questioning this assumption, '[t]he past seems less innocent; the present less sinister. One starts to appreciate the small gifts of coexistence that would have seemed utopian to our ancestors: the interracial family playing in the park, the comedian who lands a zinger on the commander-in-chief, the countries that quietly back away from a crisis instead of escalating to war.'[1]

This is an unexceptional statement, though it is more ideologically and culturally slanted than it appears to be. I, for one, agree with its main assumptions: that the present is not necessarily *more* violent than the past, and that people have tried to reduce certain kinds of violence. However, even if the present is not *more* violent than the past in some ways, it does not follow that it is any *less* violent in all ways.

No, argues Pinker, there is historical and other cognitive data that prove that the past was not just more violent than the present, but also that violence has systematically declined in history. He claims to document the decline of violence per se, not just that of some kinds of violence. There would not have been any serious problem with Pinker's thesis had it stopped at trying to prove that '[i]f we discover that violence has declined in a given people, it is because *their mode of social organization has changed,* not because the historical clock has struck a certain hour ...'[2] (italics mine). My argument here accepts this point: *the mode of social organization of a people* affects the kinds of violence (and hence the enactment of xenophobia) that is practiced by a people.

But I also argue that the violence Pinker discovers to have 'declined in a given people' is also proof of his incapacity to really understand some historical changes in the modes of 'social organization' of that people; in his case, people like him and me living in (and largely empowered by) a phase of high capitalism or 'globalization'. This extensive negotiation with 'violence' is central to any understanding of xenophobia—old or new—because xenophobia does violence to strangers. Unless we understand what forms violence might assume in specific contexts, we cannot even begin to understand xenophobia.

The Violent Cave Man

Pinker starts with some fairly acceptable propositions, for instance, with a reference to Ötzi. As Pinker puts it, in 1991, two hikers discovered a body half-buried in a melting Alpine glacier. The body, now known as Ötzi the Iceman, having graced the cover of *Time* magazine and spawned countless articles and books, is a 'celebrity'. Pinker provides a useful account of the discovery and its relevance to his project, noting the multiple evidences of physical injury on the body and skeleton of Ötzi the Iceman, including his weapons and the arrow (carrying traces of the blood of at least two people) embedded in his remains. Ötzi is estimated to have lived and died more than 5,000 years ago.

From this graphic recovery of prehistoric violence, Pinker sweeps through 'Homeric Greece', the 'Hebrew Bible', the 'Roman Empire and Early Christendom', 'Mediaeval Knights', and 'Early Modern Europe', documenting how in each case there was a high rate of violence and how, at times, we tend to forget it, partly because of our tendency to idealize the past. Pinker also talks about the decline of martial culture and domestic [male] violence, among other things. So far, there is no real problem with his thesis. One can argue, and I agree with Pinker there, that *some* kinds of violence have declined in some societies historically.

But that is not sufficient for Pinker; he wants to make a more 'scientifically' sweeping case. In the process, however, he has to be selective in contextualizing his evidence.

To begin with, while Pinker claims to talk of violence as such, he actually talks of only some kinds of violence. This is evident on the very first page, when he talks about how we do not have to worry (as much as we did in the past) about being 'abducted, raped, or killed'.[3] He proceeds to mention types of violence throughout the book, and almost always these are examples of *physical or material violence*; such references occur around 10 times in the first 25 pages of the book alone.[4] The trend continues. Violence, for Pinker, includes things like abduction, rape, and killing; it does not include salary cuts, firings, unemployment, undesirable working conditions, economically forced and demeaning labour (such as 'free' prostitution), economically influenced health conditions (such as heart attacks or obesity in some classes), demeaning behaviour, etc. We have already met General von Trotha pushing the Hereros out into the desert, where they dug holes in a bid to find water and perished, or sentencing them to hard labour in concentration camps. There is recorded evidence to believe that to many Germans, these options seemed less violent (perhaps even more civilized) than that of shooting the Hereros. Most of us would disagree; we might see little difference, today, between the two standards of violence. Such memories alone ought to make us sceptical about our own lack of violence.

Pinker's understanding of violence is obviously different from any larger philosophical conceptualization of violence. As Judith Butler puts it:

To the extent that we commit violence, *we are acting on another, putting the other at risk, causing the other damage, threatening to expunge the other.* In a way, we all live with this particular vulnerability, a vulnerability to the other that is part of bodily life, a vulnerability to a sudden address from elsewhere that we cannot pre-empt. This vulnerability, however, becomes highly exacerbated under certain social and political conditions, especially those in which *violence is a way of life and the means to secure self-defence are limited.*[5] (Italics mine)

Obviously, in a society where capital is what empowers, and most states are deeply committed to their role of creating wealth by aiding capital, it is often not necessary or even desirable to opt for physical or even material violence, that is, forms of push-out violence. Adam Smith, with typical foresight, had already seen this as early as 1776; he had argued that capitalism needs 'free' agents, people whose bodies and movements are not restricted, and commodities and skills that can be freely moved and exchanged.[6]

This, of course, was in an early phase of what I have called production-based capitalism, where the body of the worker, capitalist, adventurer, merchant, shipper, etc., could not be significantly delinked from the production of wealth and capital. This was not the kind of capitalism that we have today, where much of capital exists as numbers and not even as material cash. One does not need to physically jump a hedge in order to mint millions from hedge funds. Globalization is not as much the movement of people; this movement, as most Asians, Africans, and South Americans know, is still strictly policed unless you are well-cushioned with capital. One can argue that, in some ways, it is more controlled now— with the institutionalization of passports, better surveillance techniques, regular border controls, etc.—than it was in the pre-passport 'imperial' nineteenth or eighteenth centuries. Hence, in order to understand globalization, one has to focus not just on the number of immigrants in all societies, but also on the fact that now wealth, as numbers, does not even need to be transferred physically and materially in many cases.

To return to the kernel of Pinker's engagement with violence, one has to reiterate that Pinker is *not* wrong; he is just highly selective while appearing to be all inclusive. For instance, he may be right when he proclaims the 'reduction of violence at many scales—in the family, in the neighborhood, between tribes and other armed factions, and among major nations and states'.[7] Except that we are still talking of certain *kinds* of physical or material violence. Let alone the matter of nations and peoples, even our peaceful neighbourhoods have to be contextualized. Such relatively peaceful neighbourhoods exist on the basis of capital and wealth, and have to be conceived in the light of these three interlinked facts: they are common only in affluent countries; in less affluent countries, the peaceful neighbourhoods are mostly gated enclaves meant exclusively for very affluent people;[8] and in both these cases, others are not easily allowed into these peaceful neighbourhoods. Financial conditions or cultural reasons, including implicit xenophobia, can be employed to keep these neighbourhoods from becoming 'undesirable' and more violence-prone 'mixed neighbourhoods' and to keep refugees or immigrants from 'swamping' affluent nations. The gated neighbourhoods in India, Brazil, or South Africa are, in that sense, just local versions of Holland or Norway in the world.

Hence, while physical violence might not be as common in *such* neighbourhoods, this situation has been achieved through a degree of sublimation of violence, as well as strong controls, based on the threat of violence and the capacity to inflict it clinically and swiftly, within and without. This is violence as mediated through capital in our societies. In 'mixed neighbourhoods' this violence becomes evident—your neighbour has a Mercedes, while you have a cycle, etc.—and, hence, it can lead to a relapse into older forms of violence. You might feel driven to pound on the bonnet of his Mercedes, which, if he is stupid enough not to simply report you to the police, might tempt him to run you down on your cycle.

Strangely, early in his book, Pinker evokes a thinker whose work could have made him face up to this problem. Pinker praises Hobbes for laying out 'an analysis of the incentives of violence' in *Leviathan* (1651) that is 'as good as any today'.[9] He goes on to recapitulate that Hobbes attributed violence to 'three principal causes': competition, fear, and glory. This, Pinker claims, is as good a listing of the causes of violence as any. I happen to largely agree with Pinker here. Competition, fear, and glory, it appears, have been the major subjective explanations of violence at least in the times we are aware of, times that Marx called prehistory for largely those very same reasons. But while the explanations of violence might be the same, its forms and manifestations change character historically.

After all, the form and manifestation of *physical* violence practised by a 'caveman', say Pinker's Ötzi, is not the same as that practiced by US soldiers in Afghanistan today. While there might have been an instance or two of US soldiers clubbing or spearing a belligerent native to death, in most cases, they would have shot or bombed their opponents from a *long* distance. To move this act of violence on to other forms of violence—for instance, with the help of money (let alone capital), which would be unknown to our 'caveman'—does not take much intellectual effort.[10]

Pinker's caveman, one conjectures, and this explains some of the violence that Pinker claims had diminished, could have, if he were stronger, or if he had a supporter or two, beaten up a richer caveman and stolen his fur and spears. Our 'average man' today cannot do so; his only *legal* recourse is through capital. It is true that he is *not* beaten up physically by our richer men either, mostly; their capital does much of their work for them. They have no need or desire to beat up our 'average man'. And yet, the difference that the 'average man' now feels and sees leads him—through the mutual channels of competition, fear, and glory—to experience the emotions of, say, failure, anger, and envy. (I am not going to conjecture about the richer men.) These are also aspects of violence. Actually, in our times, in 'civilized' places, physical violence—being an outdated and 'weak' option—is mostly the prerogative of the marginalized. The empowered act through capital—and have the organized, sheathed violence of the law and its enforcement agencies to protect their privileges when the marginalized (envious! resentful! angry!) grab the outmoded weapons of *physical* violence.

It is not that violence qua violence has diminished; it has changed character and form. It has been, as Freud, whom Pinker must have read, might have put it, sublimated. To return to Pinker's Ötzi, if the body of a man from our times is recovered buried in ice some thousand years from now, surely there will be *other* signs of violence on him—not bloodied arrowheads, but perhaps the type and number (or absence) of credit cards, *brand* of clothing, evidence of or lack of starvation/obesity, sign of or lack of plastic surgery, etc.

Hobbes, as Pinker knows, believed in the fact that a 'third authority'—the Leviathan (for Hobbes, a benevolent monarchy)—with a monopoly on the use of force was the only means of curtailing anarchic violence.[11] The law itself is the body that steps in, violently, if necessary, between the anarchic revenge-based feuds of individuals and groups, and thus establishes a 'peaceful' state. But Hobbes was never under the impression, as Pinker seems to be, that this meant an evaporation of violence. (In general, Pinker's thesis is not new; not just Hobbes, but also Kant offered more complex versions of it in the past.[12])

Pinker does not define what he means by violence. If it is just physical violence that he has in mind, then he has a safer, but by no means unassailable, argument. But he talks of violence per se, while only offering examples of physical violence. One way to comprehend why he does so is to refer to his understanding of why some people react strongly to claims of diminishing violence. He attributes this to our moral psychology because 'no one has ever recruited activists to a cause by announcing that things are getting better'.[13] This seems to be quite a blinkered statement coming at the end of decades in which neo-liberalism mostly claimed that things were always getting better (all we had to do was keep spending!) and of centuries when much of European colonization was justified with reference to the civilizing mission (making *them* better!).

One of the general points made by Pinker about his purported 'decline of violence' needs to be quoted here in order to understand the dangers of this ideological blindness. Pinker writes, with some justification, that throughout history people 'began to sympathize with more of their fellow humans, and were no longer indifferent to their suffering'.[14] This, again, is true and not true; people have always sympathized with their 'fellow humans'; the ones they have not sympathized with were *not* seen as fully human, or human in the same ways as themselves, or even at all human. Rather, they were seen as monsters mostly. Early tribal societies very often seem to have considered themselves human and regarded other unknown tribes as not really human. Criminals, 'sexual deviants', witches (burnt on the stake), even apostates, etc., were not seen as fully or really or correctly human, whatever the exact historical term for 'human'—Chinese, Greek, Christian, Brahmin, Muslim, Jew, civilized, urban, European, etc.—that might have been used in particular contexts by particular peoples. Sympathy was seldom extended to strangers because their humanity could always be questioned, and hence the problems of xenophobia.

If one follows the scale and schema set out by Pinker, one automatically segregates the violence being done by 'us' (in our age, violence imposed through capital and its backers, which would include the state to a large extent) against *them* because one refuses to see it as violence. Instead, when they react or try—if one lapses into Hobbesian categories again—to compete, protect, or seek glory in their ways, this is easier to conceptualize as violence. Not being in possession of capital to the same extent, and hence not being equally backed by capital-and-property-protecting agencies, such as the state in many cases, the violence of such peoples is easy to identify as violence in Pinker's terms: physical and material violence. Hence, its (probably unintended) effect is to reduce the humanity of such peoples, by justifying violence against them and by denying them any real sympathy. A new kind of xenophobia is built into such thinking. As Judith Butler puts it in a contemporary international context:

Is our capacity to mourn in global dimensions foreclosed precisely by the failure to conceive of Muslim and Arab lives as *lives*? [...] If violence is done against those who are unreal, then, from the perspective of violence, it fails to injure or negate those lives since those lives are already negated. But they have a strange way of remaining animated and so must be negated again (and again).[15]

Of course, even without entering into a discussion of morality, such a course is not going to lead to a future of reduced violence.

Civilizing Violence

The argument continues. Pinker's chapter on the 'civilizing process' is built on some valid observations too, among these the role of what he calls 'an economic revolution' in the later Middle Ages. He has already argued that the prior movement from hunting–gathering to agriculture had led to a reduction in violence; this is a valid, if flawed, argument. It would be more correct to say that the rise of largely settled, agrarian communities led to a decline in certain types of violence, accompanied by the *creation* or *rise* of other kinds of violence. The violence of hunting and raiding was (partially) replaced by the violence of cultivation, settlement, exchange, etc. Many extant studies show how this change affected, among other things, the structures of power in families, etc. Now, Pinker argues—and he is again partly correct—that the late Middle Ages witnessed an economic revolution. He argues, correctly, that the mediaeval Christian attitude towards commerce began to change in the late Middle Ages. Pinker quotes Tuchman to this effect: 'The Christian attitude toward commerce ... held that money was evil, that according to St Augustine "Business is in itself an evil," that profit beyond a minimum necessary to support the dealer is avarice, that to make money out of money by charging interest on a loan was the sin of usury....'[16]

Pinker notes that over the next few centuries, 'money increasingly replaced barter', and this was both facilitated by, and in turn facilitated, the rise of the 'Leviathan' state (with greater centralized powers to legislate and punish). This is nothing new, of course. Thinkers on both the so-called Left and the so-called Right agree about this with astonishing frequency. Like many others, Pinker observes that the movement from land-based wealth to commodity production, commerce, and specialized labour—his theory, unlike that of Marx, fails to suggest how all this might have come about at roughly the same time—increased the possibility of creating wealth and decreased the incidence of 'violence'. Competition for land, after all, is a 'zero-sum' matter, as Pinker says; there is only that much land available (at least once a certain scale of settlement has been reached). Unlike agriculture, commerce has vaster possibilities, and also suggests other possibilities of cooperation.

While I find Pinker's account of such matters simplistic, I have no objection to its broad framework. It is largely plausible that an economic revolution of the sort outlined by Pinker (and others) did start (at least in Europe, for there is enough evidence that it started earlier or later in different parts of the world) sometime in the late Middle Ages. And perhaps it led to a reduction in certain kinds of violence, though not violence qua violence. Commercial activities included their own kinds of violence, as Shakespeare's *Merchant of Venice* indicates.[17] The early Christian prohibition against commerce and especially usury was not just blinkered; it was the logical position emanating from the conservatism of the then status quo, which was land-based and not commerce-based. Its primary purpose was to protect the status quo, but it also showed a dim and early awareness of the consequences of another possible status quo in which wealth would be delinked from material production and perhaps even value(-as-capital, in our terms) would be delinked from money. In effect, one can trace the rise of the logic of capital to this early phase—capital is not the same as money, as I argue, but it cannot be even imagined fully prior to money-based commerce. The early Christian and Muslim ('Axial-age' religions) objection to usury represents a conservative suspicion of this notion of value, value arising out of the circulation of not goods, but money. Here, we have stepped a bit closer to the concept of capital—and, from the viewpoint of early Christian thinkers, a dangerously long way from the notion of value as embedded in land and man-grown or, at worst, man-made, products.

One can argue that if the movement from hunting–gathering to agriculture was distinguished by a decline in certain kinds of physical violence, it was also marked by a rise in certain other kinds of material and symbolic violence.[18] Similarly, the movement from agriculture to commerce was distinguished by a further fall in some kinds of physical and material violence, but it was also accompanied by the rise of and/or the rise in other kinds of symbolic and material violence.[19]

Xenophobia itself alters with major historical and socio-economic changes. Just as xenophobia has changed character over time and space, violence has changed form too. Where Pinker goes wrong is in failing to identify the fact that sweeping socio-economic changes do not just lead to a decline in some kinds of violence, but *they also mark a paradigmatic shift in our perception of violence.* We come to register the old forms of violence and often fail to register the new forms because (mostly) these forms are to *our* advantage. I can illustrate this amply with historical references, but let me confine myself to Pinker's book. In one chapter, Pinker's thesis about regularly falling rates of 'violence' in history starts hiccupping when he hits the 1960s, and Pinker bravely struggles to transform the hiccups into his usual suavely academic and unintentionally ideological discourse. What was it that happened in the 1960s?

As Pinker puts it, the 'rates of violence' in the United States and in Europe

... did a U-turn in the 1960s.... European countries underwent a bounce in homicide rates that brought them back to levels they had said goodbye to a century before.... [I]n the 1960s[,] the homicide rate in America went through the roof. After a three-decade free fall that spanned the Great Depression, World War II, and the Cold War, Americans multiplied their homicide rate by more than two and a half, from a low of 4.0 in 1957 to a high of 10.2 in 1980.[20]

Pinker highlights a common demographic explanation—the 1960s was the decade when the baby-boomers became young *men*—but sets it aside, with good reason, as the explanation. He points out that the numbers of the crime boom and the baby boom do not tally, but he does highlight a new 'sense of solidarity among fifteen-to-thirty-year olds', reinforced horizontally by the rise of new media, such as radio and TV, as well as socio-cultural factors. This is a credible argument up to a point, though it begs some questions that, as we shall see, Pinker never asks.

Instead, Pinker juxtaposes what he dubs the 'decivilizing effects' against what he has already defined as the 'the civilizing process'. In general, he argues, the 'decivilizing' effects of the period—aided by such usual suspects as Marxism ('the stated enemy of the Western establishment', explains Pinker)—undercut the three main pillars of the 'civilizing process': (a) self-control; (b) societal connectedness; and (c) marriage and family life.

Once again, at first glance, Pinker seems to have a point. It is true, as he highlights, that a lot of rock music and literature, etc., in the 1960s put the onus on doing what one wanted and looked at some parts of society with suspicion: 'Don't trust anyone over thirty', advised the agitator Abbie Hoffman; 'Hope I die before I get old', sang *The Who....*'[21] Marriage and family life were also threatened. Also, one should not indulge in a vulgar leftist glorification of radicalism; keeping in mind the mimicry-influenced social nature of humans, any discourse that favours violence even in theory (or 'just words') is *likely* to lead to more actual violence too, at least in some individual cases. But having said so, one has to note what Pinker fails to see, and what is just as evident in the texts, facts, quotations, and data that he cites from the 1960s and 1970s.

One could, without condoning the violence, see the entire period from a different perspective, for example, that of young women protesting against the embedded and at times symbolic violence of male-dominated societies and family structures. It was not even Sylvia Plath, but the far from politically radical Philip Larkin, who wrote in one of his poems, 'They fuck you up, your mum and dad'. More than that, the entire feminist fight against some social and familial structures was based on a new realization of the kinds of *violence* contained in these structures. Some of it was violence so deeply internalized that, as Dale Spender has argued, it had seeped into ordinary language use as well; at its simplest, the 'semantic derogation of women' is marked by a violence in and to language that is taken for granted and that also legitimates other kinds of 'established' violence (physical, material, or symbolic) against women in society. From that perspective, it is pertinent to our understanding of the violence done to women that 'bachelor' is positively inflected and 'spinster' is not; 'lord' has preserved its original status, but 'lady' has undergone a process of 'democratic levelling' (as is also the case with 'governor' and 'governess'); and 'sir' is still a term of respect, while its equivalent, 'madam', can signify the owner of a brothel, etc.[22]

The case with other changes in the 1960s, such as the fight against racism and the civil rights movement in the USA, was similar. It is significant that the latter arose from a refusal by coloured and black citizens to be *physically* segregated on buses and elsewhere, a kind of violence that was being done to them and that was physically enforced by the authorities.[23] 'We are gonna board that old Greyhound bus/ Carrying love from town to town ...,' as the anonymous freedom song from the period, 'Keep Your Eyes on the Prize', puts it, though, of course, even here the act of boarding a bus is one of 'physical violence' against an abstract law armed with the latent violence of policing agencies.

If some feminists protested violently (and very few did), they were reacting to the growing perception that family life was largely male-centric and women were kept in place by and through institutionalized violence. If some Black activists protested violently, this was done against the institutionalized violence of Jim Crow laws and segregation. These 1960s activists (as well as non-activists, influenced by, and sometimes taking unfair advantage of, an atmosphere of justified critique) were digging, politically and at times violently, into the established violence of what Michel Foucault was to call, in a different context, the archaeology of a silence. From this perspective, it is *also* necessary to see the *rise* of violence of some kinds in the 1960s as connected to the *decline* of violence of other (often institutionalized and hegemonic) types. One may even argue that the decade of the 1960s was one of those historical periods when embedded forms of violence were revealed to a large number of people—youths, women, blacks, etc.—as not benevolent, but basically violent.

Of course, there are various other flaws in Pinker's schematic understanding of very complex factors. I will highlight only one of them: self-control. At first glance, as is the case with Pinker's 'violence', this seems a justified assumption. It does appear that people have become more 'self-controlled' over periods of history; that we, for instance, refrain from bashing in our neighbour's face when he makes a stupid remark. The idea of 'civilization' is often tied to 'self-control'. Historically speaking, the working classes, women, and non-European people were seen as largely or partly 'uncivilized' because they lacked what Pinker calls 'self-control'.

Perhaps that was so; perhaps people have become better at self-control over the centuries, led, of course, by white European men in this grand bid for an eternally progressive civilization. Except that some cavemen would have laughed at us. We cut our finger and go running for First Aid, we need anaesthetics for the slightest surgery, etc. Pinker might have forgotten this, being surrounded by urban academic types, but I grew up in a semi-rural small town in a backward part of India, surrounded by huge differences in class and modes of living. I recall that we, the richly civilized classes, found our servants lacking in 'self-control' in some areas, and they, our servants, found us lacking in 'self-control' in other areas. So, actually, we are talking of different types of self-control. It is easy, of course, to refrain from bashing in your employee's face when you have other ways in which you can express your displeasure and discipline her. The employee, on the other hand, might well be willed into self-control by the realization that the law—which does not really protect her from being fired or overworked—would take decisive action if she were to hit her boss with the fifth file that he had sent to her desk during overtime. It is necessary to note that activists and writers involved in the lives of 'subaltern' peoples often protest that even many 'progressive' and 'developmental' schemes involve gross violence, which is not registered as violence by the dominant classes.[24]

My Tolerance, Your Violence

One of the tragedies of Pinker's larger thesis is that he means well. He is not a racist or a white supremacist or a narrow champion of biological conditioning. He believes in the impact of environmental and societal factors; he believes in change for the better. Though he is often guilty of America/ Eurocentrism, this is something predicated on him by his selection of reading material and his cultural conditioning. He struggles gamely against it at times, and defuses it when he can. And yet, even at his best, his thesis suffers from a degree of selective conceptualization that is surprising in a scholar of such erudition. Take, for instance, the seemingly open and partially correct thesis in his chapter on 'the humanitarian revolution': He argues that 'beginning in the Age of Reason in the 17th century and cresting with the Enlightenment at the end of the 18th' ... '[p]eople began to *sympathize* with more of their fellow humans, and were no longer indifferent to their suffering'[25] (italics in original). Pinker argues that this was one of those trends that, across historical periods, has contributed to a decline in violence.

At first glance, this sounds plausible—and there is a germ of truth in it, at least from a Eurocentric perspective. From other perspectives (for instance, that of the non-violent philosophies of Jainism or kinds of Buddhism, all of which evolved before even the *sympathy*-based interpretations of Jesus Christ), one can argue that the Enlightenment 'sympathy' that Pinker observes was very narrow and selective; it seldom extended to savages, or animals, or, as a sect of Jains has practised down to our times, insects. While I am *not* going to beat the drum of Eurocentricism, the above observation, *minus* its accusation of Eurocentricity (which is none of my concern), does provide us with a tool to understand the limits of Pinker's thesis about a rise in sympathy.

Setting aside sects like those Jains in India who wear face- and nose-wraps to avoid inhaling even insects by mistake, it is clear that sympathy is not something simply extended; it is to a large extent determined by the categories of identification. The very etymology of 'kindness'—as having to do with your kind—is an indication of the matter. The Enlightenment expansion of European sympathy was predicated on a particular construction of the category of 'human being', to which the sympathizer belonged and other animals (sometimes even other subhumans) did not. Given his cognitivist background, I doubt that Pinker would seek to deny this; actually, the larger argument in his book even suggests this. Where I differ from him is when it comes to his assumption that we have, in some ways, overcome the conditioning of categories—categories that, I stress, are not just determined by our mental abilities, but also determined by our way of life. In that sense, Marx was at least partly right when he maintained in *The Critique of Political Economy* that it is 'not the consciousness of men that determines their existence, but their social existence that determines their consciousness'.

I will not argue the obvious fact that through much of the increasingly 'sympathetic' Age of Enlightenment, Europeans were often callously cruel to animals (because they were *not* human) and also to many non-Europeans (because, for many, these were not *really* or *sufficiently* 'human'). So the Enlightenment construction of the category 'human' was not sufficient in itself, as Jews and Gypsies were to discover with a vengeance in the Nazi period. Pichot has pointed out how the Nazi ideology accommodated or even promoted kindness to animals, especially privileged pets such as dogs, while also at the same time exterminating Jews, Gypsies, and people of 'mixed races' in the most hideous manner. Interestingly, what happened was that some people—Nazis,[26] for instance, but also European colonizers elsewhere, or upper-caste Hindus in India, or some brands of Islamists—found/find it convenient or profitable to either refuse 'humanity' to some other peoples, or to inflect 'humanity' in certain ways (Semitic/Aryan, for instance), which enabled or enable them to withhold sympathy from some groups. Unlike what Pinker seems to believe at times, the prehistoric tribe supposedly invading another tribe's ground and possibly bashing in their heads was not necessarily devoid of *sympathy*. It is more probable that it defined itself as solely or more 'human'—on the basis of whatever its category of *kind-ness* might have been.

I do not wish to argue against either the need for, or the uses of, a rational objectivity. In Coetzee's *The Lives of Animals*, Costello the novelist argues against rational thinking as not representing 'the mind of God', but just a tendency (one of many) in the mind of 'man'. This is a common relativist position, but to my mind, whether true or not, it does not render rational objectivity redundant, for 'rational objectivity' is the only ground on which we can talk together and evaluate our experiences. Other elements—emotion, faith, feeling, revelation, etc.—might or might not be true, but they are finally not conducive to a mutual discussion, and one that accords both sides equal space and authority. Claims based on faith and emotion, for instance, privilege the claimant's particular and subjective experience; they can only be accepted or rejected by others. However, having said that, I also want to highlight the dangers of an exclusive reliance on numbers and data when dealing with such a complex socio-cultural matter as 'violence' (let alone its purported decline). Pinker's thesis suffers from this excessive faith in numbers. For instance, he writes:

Now let's turn to the present. According to the most recent edition of the Statistical Abstract of the United States, 2,448,017 Americans died in 2005. It was one of the country's worst years of war deaths in decades, with the armed forces embroiled in conflicts in Iraq and Afghanistan. Together the two wars killed 945 Americans, amounting to 0.0004 (four-hundredths of a percent) of American deaths that year.[27]

But can one talk of 'American' rates of war-related violence without also factoring in the Iraqi and Afghan rates of war-related violence in a context like the above? Also, let us recall a fact often forgotten by Western historians: the discrepancy in the impact of violence because of the increasing discrepancy in the ratio of technological power. In *Capitalism in the Age of Globalization*, Samir Amin lists 'technological monopoly' and 'monopolies over weapons of mass destruction' among the five monopolies that maintain the 'present world system'.[28] Let us go just a bit further back. The Swedish historian Sven Lindqvist makes an interesting point with reference to just one historical event. He notes that while the Battle of Omdurman (1898) was often depicted in the European media as involving fierce near-combat with fanatical 'Dervishes' in Sudan, 'no Sudanese got closer than three hundred yards from the British position' because the British used advanced guns.[29] This was not unusual for the period, as a popular Hilaire Belloc poem recognized.[30] To be honest, though, the 10,000 Sudanese who were killed by British fire in the Battle of Omdurman still got a bit closer to the enemy than many of those killed in Vietnam, Cambodia, Iraq, or even Afghanistan. The ability to kill from a distance is an aspect of the decline in violence that Pinker traces, but it also involves new *methodologies* of violence. Blindness, like the one that Pinker exhibits above, brings to mind Butler's statement about now we negate the lives of others.

In Pinker's defence, it has to be said that he proceeds to talk of global rates of violence in the same paragraph: 'And in the world as a whole, the *Human Security Report Project* counted 17,400 deaths that year that were directly caused by political violence (war, terrorism, genocide, and killings by warlords and militias), for a rate of 0.0003 (three-hundredths of a percent).'[31] But again, note the nature of the violence. Pinker notices some of it, too. He tries to honestly account for this by calling it 'a conservative estimate' and multiplying it by a 'generous' 20 to include 'deaths by famine and disease': 'it would still not reach the 1 percent mark,' he states.

So perhaps there has been a decline in violence after all? I am willing to concede—I am even willing to *champion*—this conclusion for some *kinds* of violence. Pinker might have proved such a decline, by focusing on one extreme result of violence: death. But only a small percentage of all violence ends in death. Actually, with the decline in physical violence— as suggested by my reading, too—one would *expect* a decline in the number of violent *deaths*. This would be a consequence of the greater capacity of the state (or of other bodies) to both implement/carry out police violence and to concentrate its own retaliatory and 'preventive' violence (the two obviously go together). This would also be a consequence of better social organization and health and medical services; people who would have died of a stab or bullet wound just 20 years ago can be saved today, at least in affluent communities with prompt health services and good hospital facilities. But violence does not cause just deaths. Violence can be inflicted in many other ways; the caveman who could club his enemy to death does not exist (mostly) today, but the boss who can fire his employee, make her work extra hours, or cut her salary did not exist in the Stone Ages either. The raider/warlord who could rape a woman/peasant might not exist (mostly) today, but the man who extracts sexual services from a woman who needs capital and who has little else to 'sell' would also be rare in some other socio-economic historical contexts.

Pinker's 'generous' multiplication by 20 might not be all that generous. He multiplies the rate of deaths by extreme kinds of physical violence by 20 in order to account for some other kinds of material violence, such as starvation or deaths by flooding.[32]

But this logic follows no really scientific method in a world in which (according to UN statistics): more than 840 million people are malnourished; 6 million children under the age of 5 die every year as a consequence of malnutrition; 1.2 billion people live on less than a dollar a day; 12 million people die annually from lack of water and 1.1 billion do not have access to clean water; 113 million children in the developing world have no basic education; and the income of the richest 1 per cent is equal to the poorest 57 per cent.[33] Incidentally, in the USA alone,

32.9 per cent of the total population was living under the poverty line in 2001. Surely, violence has to be calculated with reference to these gross numbers, and not by 'generously' multiplying a specific and (much) delimited set of statistics by 20.

To wrap up my argument, I will return to Pinker's Ötzi-inspired archaeological evidence for falling rates of violence and look at his use of evidence from the recovery of prehistoric skeletons.[34] Pinker is aware of the two main objections raised by critics: can the paltry numbers of skeletons recovered be considered representative of large vanished populations across the centuries? And, how do we read the evidence of violence from these bits and pieces of bones?

He tries to address the first objection by combining ethnographic research with archaeological research. This is not entirely convincing to me, but I will let it rest, as I do not have any major objection to the thesis that some kinds of violence—violence by assault, which is what Pinker is actually focusing on here—might have declined in relative terms over the course of history. However, even here a number of contextual factors have been left out by Pinker. For instance, can we compare the percentage of deaths/injuries by assault in war-like situations in prehistoric times (when it is high, even if one accepts Pinker's by-no-means-foolproof combination of ethnographical and archaeological evidence) to a similar percentage of deaths/injuries in the seventeenth or the twentieth century, as Pinker does with reference to data by Quincy Wright?[35] After all, we are talking of two very *different* types of warfare and conflict: in prehistoric times, it would involve the entire tribe against another tribe; by the seventeenth century, it would involve a small percentage of the whole society (those experts of warfare: professional soldiers, hired mercenaries, etc.). Such *specialization* has increased with technological advancement:

American soldiers did not have to roam the wastes of Afghanistan as much as they had to roam the wilderness of Vietnam because of technological advancement. A technologically superior country needs fewer soldiers on the ground to fight a war today than it did even in the 1960s or, for that matter, during World War II. Obviously, the percentage of assault-type injuries will fall with technological advancement, as will the ratio of people being trained in assault and participating in it; this proves something, but nothing as sweeping or positive (alas) as Pinker wants it to prove.

Let us look more closely at these prehistoric and early skeletons with signs of assault as recovered by Pinker's archaeology. Here is what Pinker says in order to defend himself against the second objection listed above:

How can one establish the cause of death when the victim perished hundreds or thousands of years ago? Some prehistoric skeletons are accompanied by the stone-age equivalent of a smoking gun: a spearhead or arrowhead embedded in a bone, like the ones found in Kennewick Man and Ötzi. But circumstantial evidence can be almost as damning. Archaeologists can check prehistoric skeletons for the kinds of damage known to be left by assaults in humans today....[36]

It sounds convincing, doesn't it? But think again. It is true, as Pinker says, that we can *mostly* identify 'assault-type' injuries and determine whether the bone was damaged after or before the person died, at least provided that the quality of the recovered bone is fairly good. But that does *not* take us very far for a number of reasons, of which I will discuss only two. First, it is very difficult to distinguish between the types of assault-like injuries. Was the bone broken because the person was assaulted by another person, or because he was kicked by a cow, or because he fell from a cliff? One can imagine that some kinds of injuries are more likely to be sustained by people who depend on hunting–gathering than by people who depend on agriculture, and we can continue this necessary exercise in gradation to classify people who depend on commerce, and here again on different kinds of commerce, etc. (As for people who depend on the power of capital—as numbers—well, what can one say!) Second, the representativeness of the bones recovered can be difficult to ascertain. For instance, in a society that practices cremation, very little evidence of 'normal deaths' will survive; bodies from 'normal deaths' will be cremated. Hence, bones that survive in usable quantities might belong to people who died violently and whose bodies could not, or would not, be cremated. They might be victims of crime, war, or ritual sacrifice, as is the case of the Viking bog bodies that feature in Seamus Heaney's poems. Even if Pinker has his facts right, he is determined to use some facts without considering their full contextualization. Facts are always dangerous weapons, especially in the absence of context. Much violence can be done with facts and numbers now. Actually, one can argue that numbers are among the most potent weapons of violence today, partly because capitalism has led to the dominance of a kind of numerical logic. After all, capitalism, at its ideological core, is a matter of numbers.

Pinker's reliance on numbers comes at a major cost. I am not arguing for a kind of relativism or against the possibility of objectivity; I am making the different point that numbers and tables, etc., are not enough when trying to understand complex phenomena outside the ambit of the computer or the 'financial' world. Pinker, though he is always as careful as a scientist of his stature needs to be, is occasionally misled by his numbers and tables. I will give just one more example of this. Take, for instance, the rates of homicide that Pinker quotes time and again when talking of rates of violence. These rates make numerical sense, but they are misleading; in fact, the numbers, by their very nature, provide a conservative estimate of even the (very specific, delimited, and extreme) violence of homicide.

For instance, let us take a society of a hundred people in which two homicidal deaths have occurred. According to Pinker's numerical logic, this means a rate of homicide (and, hence, violence) of 2 per cent. But for those two people to have been killed, it is likely that at least one other person must have been involved. Indeed, it could be that one person killed both these two victims, or fifty people combined to do so. If we focus on the victims of homicide, we get a conservative impression of the rates of violence in this case. *Violence is not only what happens to the victims; it is also what the 'victimizers' do.* This is a fact no study of xenophobia can afford to overlook.

Pinker's numbers and his focus on certain types of physical violence do not cover all kinds of violence, let alone allow space for dealing with newly risen forms of violence. They allow us to become complacent about the kinds of violence that benefit us or do not threaten us, while at the same time using the idea of 'violence' to brand others. In this sense, Pinker's failure in his ambitious book is part of a larger failure, and closely linked to my need to think again about the violence of (new) xenophobia. It is important to stress what I hope has become evident to the reader by now: *Pinker's failure to see certain kinds of violence runs parallel to our failure to see certain kinds of xenophobia.*

What we define as violence is dependent on how we live, and this in its turn ought to be taken into consideration when discussing xenophobia. For unless we can define violence in ways that do not excuse our kinds of violence and highlight the kinds of violence of the stranger, we will always be guilty of some sort of xenophobia. This is more of an issue today, when the overlap of the changing character of capitalism and its structures of power has made it possible for different kinds of xenophobia to do different kinds of violence to strangers or foreigners. New xenophobia does not just replace old xenophobia globally; it exists along with it, and sometimes justifies its own kinds of violence with reference to the physical and material violence of old xenophobia.

6

NEW XENOPHOBIA AND OLD XENOPHOBIA

It is clear by now that, despite areas of overlap, the ways in which old xenophobia and new xenophobia operate differ in subtle ways. Let us take their presence in media discourse. One can argue that while stereotypes were more likely to be propagated directly as 'raw content' in media discourse—for instance, refer to any discussion of the 'Jewish Problem' in the nineteenth and early twentieth centuries, even in the subtle and nuanced version of the Dreyfus Affair given to us by Marcel Proust—under old xenophobia, new xenophobia is more reliant on what can be termed 'framing devices'. Stereotypes are propagated not as much by assertion as by insertion or by association.

This has been noticed in major studies such as Maxwell McCombs's *Setting the Agenda: The Mass Media and Public Opinion* (2004) and Peter Morey and Amina Yaqin's *Framing Muslims: Stereotyping and Representation after 9/11* (2011), though in slightly different terms. For instance, drawing on McCombs's study and on Edward Said's *Covering Islam: How the Media and the Experts Determine How We See the Rest of the World*, Morey and Yaqin note that:

In reportage [...] the things to look for, as much as raw content, are the contexts in which news stories are set; the juxtaposition of headline, narrative, and the accompanying photograph; the staging of the photograph; and the wider debates to which these elements refer. We argue that rather than being descriptive and neutral, such instances are almost always contained within a framing narrative whose parameters are defined by questions of belonging, 'Otherness', and threat.[1]

Even though the 'raw content' of old xenophobia is never totally absent in society (whatever might be the case of the individual), it is obvious, if one looks at the newspaper and other reports, that new forms of xenophobia often underplay the raw ('physical' or 'material') content while employing and retaining the framing devices and the framing narratives of old xenophobia. One complex example of this has been deconstructed by Jasbir K. Puar in *Terrorist Assemblages*. The construction of homonationalism, as Puar describes it, is a good indication of one of the ways in which new xenophobia differs from old xenophobia. Old xenophobia was racist, anti-Semitic, and homophobic in largely open terms; new xenophobia tries, pretends, and sometimes perhaps is genuinely *not* homophobic or anti-Semitic, even perhaps *not* racist in the old sense of a physically determined 'race' (let alone systemic, institutionalized racism), in its self-understanding.

Noting how (legitimate) gay protests against homophobia in some countries, such as Iran (and not in other countries), are connected to global politics, *Terrorist Assemblages* explores the new connections between 'sexuality, race, gender, nation, class, and ethnicity in relation to the tactics, strategies, and logistics of war machines'.[2] From our perspective, it is interesting to see how a genuine element of old xenophobia, homophobia, has been taken over by new xenophobic circles in order to legitimate a new configuration of self/other and in-group/out-group that is largely 'contingent upon ever-narrowing parameters of white racial privilege' accessed not in the openly racial terms of old xenophobia, but in the new terms of 'consumption capabilities, gender and kinship normality, and bodily integrity'.[3]

Even honestly non-xenophobic organizations can fall into this trap, as Puar demonstrates with a number of examples. For instance, the British-based queer group Outrage! displayed these placards during a rally in London at the Free Palestine rally on 21 May 2005: 'Israel: stop persecuting Palestine! Palestine: stop persecuting queers!' and 'Stop "honor" killing women and gays in Palestine.' Though informed by an honourable intention to protest against both Islamophobia and homophobia, Puar notes that this combination of placards

> [...] unfortunately reaffirms the modernity of Israel and Judaism and the monstrosity of Palestine and Islam. Delineating Palestine as the site of queer oppression—oppression that is equated with the occupation of Palestine by Israel—effaces Israeli state persecution of queer Palestinians. Israeli state persecution of queer Israelis—because Israel is hardly exempt from homophobic violence towards its own citizens regardless of religious or ethnic background—is erased in this trickle-down model of sloganeering. This dialectical analogy, whereby the persecution of Palestinians by Israel is 'like' Palestinian persecution of queers, does a tremendous disservice to the incommensurate predicaments at stake and refuses any possible linkages between the two, indeed refuses that one form of oppression might sustain or even create the conditions of possibility for the other.[4]

In terms of our thesis here, it is also evident how the new stranger sanctioned by new xenophobia—in this case, the Palestinian—is implicitly and explicitly portrayed as practicing a bodily located violence—'honour' killing, the persecution of gay men and women, etc.—while the more normative 'ally' (Israel) practices, at worst, a lopsided form of an abstract violence, that of and against a 'nation'. Puar exposes the devices by which a *normatization* of queerness is both constructed and used against a new xenophobic target that, in the folds of its abstraction, mystifies and obscures 'the primary beneficiaries of this epistemological project: European subjectivities'.[5]

This brings us to one of the most prominent problems faced by anti-xenophobia and anti-racism groups today: the *difference* between old racist/xenophobic parties and many new Rightist parties; what Roger Griffin aptly terms 'fascism's new facelessness'.[6] With equivalent versions existing in countries as varied as Switzerland, Holland, Denmark, and Norway, this is best illustrated with the example of the English Defence League (EDL). As Arun Kundnani shows in an excellent paper, EDL— like similar new Rightist groups and leaders elsewhere (such as the Flemish nationalist Vlaams Belang party or Pim Fortuyn in Holland)—often goes to great lengths to distance itself from old forms of racism, homophobia, and anti-Semitism, all of which were staples of the old Right (and of Nazism). They even, as is also the case with mainstream Rightist parties like the nationalist Danish People's Party, distance themselves from neo-Nazism, at least in some public pronouncements. While there are obvious elements of relapse and overlap—such as the tendency to visit the sins of some 'Muslim' terrorists on all Muslims, nationalist references to secular 'crusades', and the existence of a commonality of supporters with old Rightist and old xenophobic (including Nazi) sympathies—it would be a mistake to consider these new Rightist groups as simply masquerading and pretending, of throwing dust into the public eye while basically recycling neo-Nazi ideologies. Kundnani is correct in stating that 'it would be wrong to see the EDL as simply a mask for more familiar forms of far-Right, racist politics. Equally, it would be a mistake to think that the EDL's distinction between moderate and extremist Muslims, even when properly upheld, does not involve it in a politics of race.'[7]

Kundnani notes that most discussions of the EDL consider whether it is another right-wing and extremist organization, which opportunistically employs popular concern over Islamist radicalism 'to mask an old-fashioned racist and violent politics, or whether it represents, at least for some supporters, a legitimate attempt to oppose totalitarian Islamism'.[8] He adds,

[i]n a report for the liberal think-tank *Demos*, for example, Jamie Bartlett and Mark Littler conclude that, though some EDL supporters use opposition to militant Islam as 'a cover for more sinister or intolerant views,' many are genuine anti-extremists who carefully distinguish between moderate and extremist Muslims. [...] Labour party advisor Maurice Glasman seems to agree with this position, saying in an interview with *Progress* magazine in April 2011 that we should listen to the supporters of the EDL.[9]

From the perspective of this study, the complexity of such new Rightist ideological moorings is useful; it helps to place these new Rightist groups in the interface between old xenophobia and new xenophobia. This interface is best illustrated by pointing out how their rhetoric slips into old forms of a body-centred xenophobia and also, sincerely, employs elements of new xenophobia, that feature the feared stranger who is guilty of excesses of physical differentiation and bodily violence. I will illustrate both with examples from texts by EDL, by italicizing and underlining the crucial words:

A. Traces of Old Xenophobia:
    In the last 66 years we as a *nation*, as a *race* have had our _national identity_ stolen from us by politicians who have _forced_ us to accept _multiculturalism_. They have and still are practicing _cultural genocide_ on their own people, despite warnings that we will not accept it. They have _forced_ us to accept the dilution of our heritage and

history by the implementation of <u>laws which will stop us from rising up, even if that's just to voice an opinion</u>. Any <u>action</u> which has the aim or effect of depriving us of our *integrity as distinct peoples*, or of our *cultural values* or *ethnic identities*. Any form of *population transfer* which has the aim or effect of <u>violating</u> or undermining any of the rights of the *native or indigenous people*. Any form of *assimilation or integration by other cultures or ways of life* imposed on us by legislative, administrative or other measures is *cultural genocide*.[10] (Italics and stresses mine)

B. Traces of New Xenophobia:

'Muslim Bombers Off Our Streets.' 'Extremist Muslims Go to Hell.' 'British Voters Say No to Sharia Law.' 'Long Live the Free.'[11]

What is interesting about these two selections is how, in A, the EDL slips into old forms of a body-centred xenophobia, with its stress on blood, inheritance, heredity, genetics, etc., while constantly struggling to sublimate these factors into the realm of culture. If one looks at the words put in *italics*, one detects a slippage into old Rightist/racist/xenophobic understandings of inherited and body-based elements; 'nation' slips into 'race', and 'ethnic identities' and terms like 'native' and 'indigenous' return the discourse to an understanding of biologically inherited differences. Along with these we have words and phrases, the ones <u>underlined</u> and *italicized*, that show a degree of vacillation, often trying to reframe, and sometimes reframing, old xenophobic grievances in new sublimated (mostly 'cultural') terms. The term 'cultural genocide', with its coupling of an idealist construction with physical death, is significant in this context. Finally, the words or phrases that have been only <u>underlined</u> above show how the EDL positions itself as a party of sublimated protest—abstractly 'voicing an opinion'—that is physically 'forced' by the legislative, administrative, and other measures of pro-multiculturalism politicians into marginalization. To understand this final element, it is important to see it in the light of the 'Muslims' that EDL claims to be opposing. In B, for instance, the EDL pointedly refers to Muslims as practitioners of a bodily impacted extremism positioned or juxtaposed against the ideal, abstract values, such as 'freedom', of the English.

What we witness is a complex interweaving of old xenophobic elements with new xenophobic ones. The threat of a physical difference—a tribal, genetic identity that can be inherited, not cultivated—lurks in the background, but is often expressed, and sometimes realized, in more sublimated terms. Here the notion of culture, a word whose etymology is revealing, is particularly useful because while it is widely understood as not necessarily biological, it still retains vestiges of its meaning in phrases like 'preparing a physical culture'. But this attempted freeing of the body from marks of differences—which is, as argued, perfectly in keeping with the increasing abstraction of capital in First World spaces—is posited against the captivity of the body in those 'other' spaces that have to be opposed. Hence, new xenophobia does not oppose physical difference; it opposes any manifestation of physical difference. Jews do not have to wear a Star of David, but Muslims cannot build minarets or dress in certain kinds of clothes in public spaces.

Government policies in almost all rich countries reflect this kind of xenophobia; immigrants are discriminated against, openly, not on the basis of their appearances, but on the basis of their 'qualifications'. Again, this is done in increasingly abstract terms, as Roemer, Lee, and van der Straeten point out: 'law and order', architectural heritage, democracy, etc.

This brings us back to a major and elided contradiction running through the entire process, which I have to return to repeatedly in this part of the book: globalization has left capital more free to traverse the globe than ever before, but this has not—and indeed *cannot*, if welfare and prosperity are to be maintained at the currently high levels in the gated First World countries of the world—left labour with an equivalent, or even vaguely comparable, mobility across borders that matter. This basic contradiction—that the prosperity of the First World depends on the freedom of 'global' capital while its privileges depend on the control of global labour—has translated into new xenophobia that legitimates the miniscule minority from the Third World with access to global capital and legislates abstractly to deny access to the vast majority. The rationale for this discrimination is perforce abstract (partly in reaction to old xenophobia, which can also conveniently provide a rationale for the construction of the odious stranger now), even though it often overlaps with old targets of xenophobia for historical and 'cultural' reasons.

Under new xenophobia, the stranger—always constructed by every kind of xenophobia—is not just the 'outsider'. If the feared and detested stranger in ancient Greek city states was by definition the non-urban outsider, the feared and detested stranger in our stock-market-linked cities is the man or woman whose body intrudes into and disrupts the smooth circulation of the abstract power of capital. The stranger is constructed increasingly as a bodily being whose physical tyranny runs against the idealist nature of our commerce and its self-claimed values: freedom, democracy, equality, etc. Hence, the stranger to be feared is, as even Pinker's reading of violence unwittingly suggests, the person who imposes bodily constraints on himself and others, either in the shape of dress, dietary practices, ritual-related behaviour, or even architectural elements. In this sense, the old xenophobic revulsion from Jews as 'circumcised' is not necessarily the same as the new xenophobic distaste of Muslims as people who *circumcise* their children.

The Old Xenophobia of Asia and Africa

We have seen that new xenophobia can draw upon old xenophobia in complex ways, as indicated earlier in the case of homophobia. It does not just overlap with and differ from old xenophobia, but it also draws upon forms of old xenophobia by using the 'other' as justification. One way to examine the dialectical complexity of this reaction is to turn away from Europe and America, and look at the so-called Muslim world.

It is in this context that we have to return to political Islam today, remembering well that the capitalist modes of production are un(der)developed in most Muslim countries. These countries (with the partial exception of a country like Malaysia, which was held up as such a good 'Muslim' example during the Afghanistan war) also have a very small bourgeoisie in general; the Muslim bourgeoisie in India might well exceed those of all the Arab countries combined. The affluence of some Arab countries is misleading, as these nations benefit from the accident of the extraction of a raw commodity and its developed exploitation by global/Western capitalists: crude oil. Such countries lack wide and significant embourgeoisment, both in material and cultural terms.

This lack of developed capitalist modes of production has 'local', 'national', and 'global' reasons, of which the most important might well be the nature of capitalism itself. As Samir Amin notes in *Capitalism in the Age of Globalization*, favourable conditions, like the massive accumulation of capital permitted by conquest and/or colonization as well as Europe's ability to get rid of its surplus population in a crucial period, have not been available to the rest of the world. In the present, too, as Amin notes, most of the immense amounts of floating capital in the world seeks investment by roaming from one financial metropolis to another, hardly ever paying a visit to the Third World, and that too mostly as short-term investment.

But it is not my thesis here that the 'reactionary' and at times old xenophobic tendencies in many Muslim societies today are the reflection of their pre-capitalist or quasi-capitalist status. Such a thesis would falsely return us to the past as providing a simple and direct explanation of the present. Moreover, such an explanation would also obscure the 'globalizing' nature of capitalism today. Capitalism touches almost everyone in the world today, though, of course, it does not touch everyone in the same way or to the same extent.

What I wish to highlight is the fact that Muslim countries, along with other 'Third World' and 'Fourth World' countries, have undeveloped or underdeveloped modes of capitalist production. This, combined with the lack of historically favourable conditions for the development of Europe-style capitalism, leaves these countries with a small and insecure bourgeoisie, which does not have the success or wealth to incorporate or force the other classes to accept its hegemony. In these countries, the local bourgeoisie has failed to achieve the building of a modern self-reliant economy. This local/national bourgeoisie lacks the courage and the wealth to really compete with the international bourgeoisie in economic terms, and is thus confined to only one half of its role as a *national* bourgeoisie: collaboration with the *international* bourgeoisie. However, in keeping with the nation-state-based political structure of the post-war international community and its own self-definition, this local bourgeoisie can only exist as a national bourgeoisie if the nation state continues to exist—and to exist simultaneously with it. For that, the national bourgeoisie needs both the resources that it can obtain from the international bourgeoisie—by trading, trafficking, or begging—and, above all, it needs to keep on differentiating itself *symbolically* from the international bourgeoisie. This differentiation can only be made in the symbolic sphere because its inability to compete with the international bourgeoisie deprives the national bourgeoisie of both hegemony in the nation state and a plausible appearance of material or economic differentiation.

It is here that 'Islam' steps into the picture in many Muslim countries. Its appeal to sections of the immigrant population is consolidated by the fact that religious identity, unlike national identity, exceeds geographical borders—hence, religion becomes doubly attractive to many immigrants in the West, who are caught outside or between national borders. This, however, is not just a 'Muslim' characteristic. 'Hinduism' is being used in similar ways in India, a usage altered slightly by the fact that India has a relatively large bourgeoisie, and historical Hinduism has a different history and genesis from historical Islam.

The game that has been played in most Muslim countries is a double-edged one. On the one hand, the bourgeoisie and the traditional elite seek and often obtain many of the benefits of capitalism. On the other hand, the people live under conditions of un(der)developed modes of capitalism. This quasi-capitalist state of economic activity to which most of the population is confined, due to the failures of the national bourgeoisie *and* the structure of (global) capitalism, necessitates a corresponding 'quasi-capitalist' symbolic world, which is largely achieved with the help of a reductive reading of Islam. For reasons of prestige (borrowed from the 'past') and availability, this 'quasi-capitalist' symbolic world has to rely heavily on certain 'pre-capitalist' tendencies that appear most opposed to the capitalist symbolic world; of these, a body-centred nexus of power is the core.

Apart from the logic of its evocation, this also enables the elite to profit from its complicity in global capitalism while keeping the people not only alienated from the partly democratic tendencies of capitalism (fetishized into the 'West' in, at times, old xenophobic terms in many Muslim countries),[12] but also singularly unable to comprehend the real structures of their oppression. Instead of partly competing and partly collaborating with the global capitalist (as it would have if it had been a full and vigorous national bourgeoisie), the Muslim national elite in most Muslim countries simply collaborates with the global capitalist in material terms while appearing to provide an alternative to the people in symbolic terms. Saudi Arabia is the most extreme example of this. This suits *all* the elites and the bourgeoisie concerned most of the time, for the fully abstract nature of capital today makes it more strategic for the global capitalist to keep away from territorial entanglement (which, by the way, also helps us understand the kinds of wars grudgingly waged by the USA in recent years).

Islamic fundamentalist parties are a spin-off from this game, a game that (it must be stressed) suits dominant business and political interests in the 'West'. Even when they end up challenging the legitimacy of the government of a Muslim country, fundamentalist parties do not really upset the capitalist apple cart. Reacting to the abstract structures of power under capitalism, the leaders of these fundamentalist parties try to 'restore' what they consider Islamic, inevitably stressing the structures of power that impact directly on the body under pre- or quasi-capitalist conditions. (The Taliban was but the expression of this oppositional logic taken to its limit; Saudi Arabia continues to be its institutionalized face.) The valid attempt to resist the abstract structures of power under capitalism leads to not a (revolutionary) re-evocation of the body under changed conditions, but rather to a defensive/conservative/reactionary attempt to preserve the body under old pre-capitalism-like structures of power. From a radical perspective, the main problem with this oppositional formulation is its inability to fight the real structures of power under global capitalism. It can only indulge in pointless physical/material violence, like the bombing of the World Trade Center (WTC) building in New York City, violence that, if anything, enables capitalist ideologues to consolidate their hold on abstract power.

Here I should spell out the hitherto implicit fact that I am *not* indulging in the vulgar Marxist tendency of blaming exploitation simply on the 'exploitative nature' of an evil elite. The bourgeoisie or the elite in Muslim (and Third World) countries is partly forced by the very logic of global capitalism, including capitalism's imbrication and its tensions with the nation state, to seek to establish its hegemony over the other classes by means of the only thing it can press into service: the evocation of a past that, in its pre-capitalist tendencies, might serve as an (ineffective) critique of capitalism (or, more exactly, the capitalist 'West'). Had the Muslim or Third World bourgeoisie been successful in capitalist terms (something precluded by the very mechanism of historical capitalism), this would not have been necessary to the same extent. And had revolutionary critiques, such as radical socialism or Marxism, been allowed to flourish in these countries, there might have been other alternatives to this recourse to an Islam defined by and 'refined' into its most body-impacted, pre-capitalist elements.

The point to note, however, is that the 'past' that comes into being due to the nexus of these interests and forces has been created very much in the present. This is underlined by the technical and vocational education of many supporters of Islamic (and Hindu) fundamentalism, the highly political character of much of Islamic (and Hindu) fundamentalism, as well as the fact that Islamists are not really interested in writing exegeses of the Quran, and Hindu fundamentalists tend to turn the Ramayana into a pulp television serial rather than study the original in Sanskrit. Features of old xenophobia (even largely borrowed ones, such as anti-Semitism in recognizably early twentieth-century European terms in the case of Islamism) come with this reworking of the past in a contemporary context, a context in which Muslim countries are largely still embedded in forms of classical or production-based capitalism even when, at times, their elites share and indulge in global high capitalism.

Islamists and their critics in the 'West' use terms of definition that play out this contrast between capitalist and pre-capitalist structures of power, which is often translated into the resistance of the body to abstract capital, if you are anti-capitalist or anti-West;[13] and the freedom of the body from the tyranny of society/religion, which is the dominant view in the capitalist 'West'. The intense 'Muslim' suspicion of the 'West' is not just due to the lack of self-criticism in the Muslim world that Salman Rushdie has castigated in a recent article in the *Guardian*. Actually, from at least the day in 1099 when Abu Sa'ad al-Harawi burst into the diwan of al-Mustazhir Billah decrying Muslim decadence and weakness in the face of the advancing Crusaders, Muslim communities have indulged in as much (reactionary or revolutionary) self-criticism as any other community. The Muslim suspicion of the 'West' is due to a garbled realization by the average Muslim of the structures of power under global capitalism, structures that touch him very differently from how they touch Rushdie or an Arab sheikh, or even a humble white clerk in London.

This is a mutual failure. While the capitalist 'West' and many members of the bourgeoisie elsewhere often perceive the bodily structures of power that are made to dominate 'traditional Islam' with great repulsion, they also fail to address their own abstract structures of power. A minor proof of the latter is the fact that the debt of the peripheral economies grew from US$ 900 billion in 1982 to US$ 1,500 trillion in the late 1990s, of which half was expended on interest. One indication of the imbrications of these mutual failures is the sustenance that new xenophobic tendencies in the 'free' West derive from the cultivation (and, in the case of rising anti-Semitism and extreme homophobia, partly plagiarism) of old xenophobic tendencies elsewhere. However, what I have said of dominant aspects of Islamism also applies to many non-Muslim reactionary groups elsewhere: for instance, regardless of what we may think of the ideas of the Tea Party in USA, its ground support is built on the perception, not entirely wrong in the financial context of 'globalization', that 'Washington and Wall Street are in bed together'.[14]

Returning to coloured immigrants, it needs to be conceded that *some* conservative migrants do bring with them their own baggage of old xenophobic perceptions, determined by ingrained theories of blood, descent, race, lineage, etc., which have not been fully abstracted by liberal capitalism and its ethos. But not all immigrant attempts at 'strong identity politics' should be reduced to just this element. Charles Taylor talks about the fact that while migrants still want to assimilate into their new countries, they increasingly want to do so on their own terms:

The earlier sense of unalloyed gratitude toward the new countries of refuge and opportunity, which seemed to make any demand to recognize difference quite unjustified and out of place, has been replaced by something harder to define. One is almost tempted to say, by something resembling the old doctrine which is central to many religions, that the earth has been given to the human species in common. A given space doesn't just unqualifiedly belong to the people born in it, so it isn't simply theirs to give.[15]

If Taylor is right and there is this return, then it needs to be added that this is partly different from the old religious conceptions. I would argue that this new feeling, if it exists, is a contorted understanding of the obscured relationship between labour and capital. The fact that 'your' capital can penetrate 'my' world with relative impunity gives 'me' the right to bring 'my' labour past your border checkpoints; it is in the physical enactment of my labouring body that 'I' can, symbolically, resist the power of 'your' abstract capital that forces 'me' to be where 'I' am and/or denies 'me' the options of mobility that 'you' have. Just as this physical enactment becomes an aspect of oppositional politics in the abstract power networks of high capitalism, those who have deeply internalized these abstract networks also tend to construct violence as solely a *physical* irruption.

This can also happen in spaces where one has an extreme intermingling of high capitalism and pre-capitalist or quasi-capitalist lifestyles. Centralist Turkey has, at times, indulged in a similar framing of Kurds. In India, for instance, the often upper-caste and always upper/middle-class distaste of Maoist and related revolutionary politics by the lower castes and classes and aboriginal peoples is often constructed along a similar divide; globally capitalized Indians contrast themselves favourably against the physical violence of these other Indians, violence that, in extreme versions, 'delegitimizes' their grievances. The Indian case is a reminder of the fact that what we are dealing with is a reflection of the changing nature of capitalism, and not just cultural factors, such as Eurocentricism.

The New Legislation of New Xenophobia

Old xenophobia framed laws that discriminated on the basis of visible differences, even as it sought abstract justification for such uneven structures of power. Hence, Social Darwinism; hence, racism; hence, the ethnic/linguistic fervour of nationalisms. If differences were not visible, or readily visible, old xenophobia legislated to make them visible. The Nuremberg Laws (1935) of the Nazis serve as the easiest illustration of this legislative trend of old xenophobia. Enacted largely to define Jewishness more than it had been possible in the past, and as a follow-up to an existing Nazi boycott of Jewish business, these laws were clearly focused on making difference visible by assuming a fraudulent, naturalized biologism. Fuzzy border/contact areas were excised, as in the definition that a German was someone with four German (or 'kindred') grandparents, while a Jew was someone with three or four Jewish grandparents; a person with one or two Jewish grandparents was a 'Mischling' or cross-breed, and the Nazis made extensive efforts to weed out such 'race bastards' too. This enforced visibility of the stranger under the Nuremberg Laws extended from a ban on German–Jewish marriages and sexual relations to an insistence that Jews could not use German national colours and had to be identified by their own 'national' colours.

Most anti-xenophobic laws today are designed to cope with this old xenophobic trend of segregating and tagging strangers. And, to the credit of past legislators, some of it has had positive consequences. But, as seen above, the nature of the New Right has changed in keeping with the structure of high capitalism. Hence, as ECRI puts it in its annual report of 2005, '[t]oday, the idea of "culture" appears to increasingly replace the idea of race'. Or, as Kundnani further stresses the matter, in recent years the concept of racism has been turned on its head: 'It was no longer a question of the ways in which society systematically excluded particular groups and thus set in train a process of ghettoization. It was supposed, instead, that non-white groups themselves refused to integrate and thus made themselves strange to whites, some of whom then became hostile.'[16]

While I have not attempted to deny the existence of xenophobia—in old or new xenophobic shapes—among non-white individuals and in non–First World countries, Kundnani is right in noting and critiquing this change, which (to underline an obvious point) again illustrates the differences between enactments of old and new xenophobia.

At the root of such a perception of 'new immigrants' and the perversion of racism (which is turned from an institutional and systemic matter, as illustrated in an earlier chapter, into a personal prejudice) lie some very old structures of occlusion and confusion. For instance, scholars like the historian Walter Laqueur try to explain the seemingly greater prevalence of xenophobia in Western Europe today by adducing a relative paucity of xenophobia when immigrants came to Europe in the nineteenth century too. Laqueur presents three broad arguments for this perceived difference (between a nineteenth-century Europe that was purportedly not anti-migrant and a twentieth-century Europe that became increasingly anti-migrant):

1. '[T]he scale of immigration. Only tens of thousands came to Western Europe 100 years ago, not millions.'
2. 'They made great efforts to integrate socially and culturally. Above all, they wanted to give their children a good secular education at almost any price. The rate of intermarriage was high within one generation, and even higher within two.'
3. 'No one helped them: There were no social workers or advisors, no one gave them housing at low or no rent, and programs such as Sure Start (a British equivalent of Head Start) and "positive discrimination" had not yet been invented. There were no free health-service or unemployment benefits.'[17]

But, advertently or inadvertently, such arguments are based on large areas of evasion, ideological blind-spots, and faulty contextualization. Some of these can be listed as below:

With reference to point 1: The nineteenth century, as well as centuries just previous to it, were also periods of emigration in Europe; millions of Europeans left Europe or were shipped out (as prisoners, etc.) to populate other continents.[18] The peoples of these other continents were not consulted on this, and were often significantly marginalized in the process, permanently in America and Australia.[19] The fact that Europeans resented immigrants 'less'—if it is true (which is doubtful given the rich history of internal conflicts in Europe, which, despite a period of relative peace, led to the so-called World War I)—surely had to do something with the fact that they were also emigrating on largely their own terms in the same period. Moreover, the claim that fewer numbers of immigrants were entering Europe is misleading; the population of Europe in 1850 was 200 million and the world population was around 1,200 million, while the current population of Europe is about 750 million and the world population is around 7,000 million. Surely, the way to talk about immigration, then and now, is to consider the ratio of immigrants to native populations, and not to compare the number of immigrants in 1850 to the number in 2010. In other words, the equivalent of one immigrant in Europe in 1850 would be almost four immigrants today in terms of European population growth, and it would be higher in terms of world population growth. An exact indicator would need to factor in both of these indexes.

With reference to point 2: The supposed integration of nineteenth-century immigrants is misleading, even if it were true internally (which is doubtful); it might well be the effect of hindsight (these nineteenth-century immigrants appear to have integrated better today because we are looking at them from across a century, by which time their descendants have obviously integrated) and distance (the further away we move, the less we can see the smaller differences and conflicts). Moreover, it does not include slaves, their descendants, and coloured immigrants, who seldom 'intermarried' into Europe in any significant numbers. Laqueur turns a stone phase to the racism implicit in his remark about intermarriage. He also does not take into account that as late as the nineteenth century different individuals married or did not marry on the basis of indicators other than those of nationality: for instance, Protestants from (incipient) nations or cultures would be more likely to intermarry one another than to marry a Roman Catholic, and an upper-class American was more likely to marry an upper-class English person than a coal miner or a washerwoman. Even regarding racism, there is a good argument (at least with respect to India and Indians in Great Britain) that the late eighteenth century was less racist and hence slightly more open than the nineteenth century.[20] Hence, Laqueur's remark is blind to certain kinds of immigration and quite dishonestly eludes ethnic, racial, and similar prejudices of the time. Similarly, the claim that immigrants in the nineteenth century wanted to give their children a 'good secular education' is strangely blind to the fact that in nineteenth-century Europe all good—including so-called secular—education had a heavily Christian character.[21]

But the most remarkable occlusions, and the ones most pertinent to my thesis, are found in **point 3**. Obviously, what Laqueur is talking about is a First World welfare state. By definition, this is a European state whose welfare structures are based on previous centuries of colonial affluence and current decades of capitalist dominance. The point of such welfare states has been to provide a safety net to national labour, while enabling national capital to profit internationally. Evidently, this happens in a 'free' capitalist world, where goods, labour, and capital are supposed to move without hindrances. So, actually, what Laqueur and others are objecting to is the penetration of labour from *elsewhere* into such artificially protected social welfare states, whose affluence continues to depend on their dominance as states and on their being the preferred locations of capitalists under 'global' high capitalism. (I will omit commenting on the obvious liberal ideological bias of point 3; it need only be read in conjunction with a speech by a hardcore Republican in the USA for its ideological underpinnings to become clear.)

Evidently, such arguments serve basically as justification of or as incentive for new xenophobic laws, while sometimes genuinely opposing forms of old xenophobia (among whites or non-whites, Europeans or non-Europeans). The problem with these laws is that, unlike the laws of old xenophobia, they work in the abstract. They presuppose some abstract, 'universal', and ideal causes, justified in themselves, that perform two kinds of occlusion (quite similar to the occlusions of Laqueur's kind of argumentation): (a) they occlude the fact that they afflict some people (undesirable strangers) more than other people; and (b) they are based on old xenophobic assumptions about these undesirable strangers, which are not even enunciated or recognized consciously.

Take, for instance, these recent rules passed in Denmark to regulate marriages:

1. The 24-Year Rule: 'In order to qualify for family reunification, both the spouse living in Denmark and the foreign spouse must normally be older than 24. However, an application for family reunification can be submitted when the younger spouse is 23½ years old.' [22]

2. The Self-Support Requirement: 'Normally, it is a requirement that your spouse/partner in Denmark is able to support him/herself.

   This means that your spouse/partner in Denmark may not have received public assistance under the terms of the Active Social Policy Act (lov om aktiv socialpolitik) or the Integration Act (integrationsloven) for the past three years prior to your application for family reunification being processed by the Immigration Service.

   It makes no difference how long a person has received public assistance if it was received in the past three years. Even short periods on social benefits ('kontanthjælp') may result in your application for family reunification being turned down.' [23]

3. The Immigration Test: 'Applicants for family reunification who submit their applications after 15 May 2012 are not

required to pass an immigration test (*indvandringsprøven*). Instead, applicants must pass Danish as a second language test. Read more about the Danish test. You must normally pass the immigration test in order to be granted a residence permit on the grounds of family reunification with your spouse/partner in Denmark. In certain situations, you can be exempted from taking the immigration test. Furthermore, citizens of Australia, Canada, Israel, Japan, New Zealand, Switzerland, South Korea and the USA are exempt from taking the immigration test.'[24]

4. The Attachment Requirement: 'The connection requirement will be waived if the spouse living in Denmark has had **Danish citizenship for more than 26 years**.

   The same applies if the spouse living in Denmark was born and raised in Denmark or arrived in Denmark as a young child and **has resided in Denmark legally for more than 26 years**.

   If the applicants are required to meet the connection requirement, family reunification can initially only be granted if *their combined connection to Denmark is greater than their combined connection to another country*.'[25] (Bold in original; italics mine)

Such 'new' legislation presents a number of fascinating aspects that underline my argument about new xenophobia. They are worded in an abstract manner ('universal'), though their implementation has far more *particular* aspects or effects than the wording or theory suggests. Rule 1 discriminates between nationals and foreigners; obviously, you do not need to wait for marriage until you are 24 if both you and your partner are Danish. This is in keeping with a certain return of old xenophobic sentiments in abstract forms; for instance, the belief that somehow the citizen is entitled to preferential treatment despite the rhetoric of human rights, either in the name of entitlement or of protection. It is a belief that was once very common. Given the fact that only a small percentage of marriages to foreigners run the risk of being forced or even arranged marriages, this discriminatory law reminds one, at a diluted level, of the logic behind Nazi concentration camps: 'Better to put ten innocents behind barbed wire than to let one real enemy escape.'[26] Similarly, the privileging of one's own citizens in matters of human rights is reminiscent of a similar, though stronger, claim of ingrained privilege made for various races, nationalities, and volk in the early twentieth century. But these are matters that relate rule 1 to the history of what I have termed old xenophobia; they are based on an obvious difference being made between nationals and foreigners (though, bear in mind, that 'nationals' and 'foreigners' are highly abstract terms). This rule is revealed as an aspect of new xenophobia only when you look at what is not being said. Given the fact that European Union legislation, as well as dual agreements with (and in recognition of the economic status of) First World countries like the USA, Canada, Australia, and even Japan, allow their citizens to move, work, and settle with relative freedom in Denmark, rule 1 is basically applicable to Third World countries, whose citizens have less chance to enter Denmark or work there. Of course, these targets overlap with the past targets of old xenophobia: the old 'coloureds' from Africa, Asia, and South America. But not only has this been put in highly abstract terms, some avenues are made relatively open to highly trained people from the globalized minorities of these debarred labouring spaces, such as doctors from India or Brazil. Rule 3 operates with a similar logic; it just 'happens to' apply more to people from the Third World and to coloured

people than to people from the EU, who can work and stay in
Denmark for long periods without needing to emigrate or to
take immigration tests. In this case, the globalized abstract-
capital logic of the law is made obvious by attaching a seemingly
arbitrary list of countries whose citizens do not have to take an
immigration test that, some Danish journalists have claimed,
many ethnic Danes would have trouble passing: 'Australia,
Canada, Israel, Japan, New Zealand, Switzerland, South Korea,
and the USA.' Seemingly arbitrary, I wrote, but this is not really
so if you keep my larger argument in mind, and think of the
trajectory of new xenophobia: Israel, South Korea, and Japan
are arguably *the* non-white nations most deeply entrenched in
high capitalism.

That we have moved into a new realm of abstract economic
xenophobia is illustrated by rule 2, where *impoverished Danes*
are discriminated against. There is something endearingly
genuine about the double-speak on race and colour in the laws
of new xenophobia; this is a *genuine* dislike of those who do not
belong or contribute to the realms of high capital, even when
they share one's own race or nationality. Interestingly, the New
Right, such as the Danish People's Party, despite its pseudo-
socialist discourse of championing marginalized Danes, is not
concerned about such discrimination.

Rule 4 is even more interesting. It posits a 26-year residence
in Denmark, which means that it basically privileges people
born in Denmark, at least as far as their first marriage or
partnership is concerned. The vast majority of young people
enter their first significant relationship in their early or mid-
twenties. This rule obviously privileges ethnic Danes. One can
take the argument further and say that this is a rule biased
against women; even in Denmark most women are a bit
younger than their male spouses. This means that if you are

a man, you have a statistically better chance of bringing your partner into the country than vice versa. This is undergirded by the rider that 'their combined connection to Denmark should be greater than their combined connection to another country'. This rider also abstractly discriminates against Danish citizens of non-Danish 'ethnic' origin, as these people, even if born in Denmark, might have spent some years in other countries, the countries of one or both of their parents. (It need hardly be pointed out that this rule, too, is easier to overcome in practice if your spouse/partner belongs to an EU nation than if s/he belongs to Nigeria or India.)

The Øresund Bridge, a century-long dream for Swedes and Danes achieved in the twenty-first century, is a 16-km-long motorway and railway link that spans the strait, uniting the tip of Sweden and the most commercial island of Denmark into a large commercial and cultural region. It now takes about half an hour by train to travel from Copenhagen to the next major town in Sweden, Malmö. Among the people who commute both ways are some young men and women. You can see them, at times, commuting as couples. Indeed, these are couples, and only one of them is Danish. The other one is usually not Swedish either. In most cases, it is a non-European or an East European. The reason why they live in Malmö is simple; the above-mentioned and similar 'marriage laws' in Denmark make it very difficult for poor Danes to get their partners to join them. These laws also make it difficult for affluent Danes to get their partners to join them, particularly if the partner is not from a developed Western country. These rules are not discriminatory in an old xenophobic sense, but they affect some strangers more than they affect other strangers. Many of the strangers affected by these rules would have been affected by the prejudices of old xenophobia, too, except that most such prejudices—overt racism, for instance—are illegal in Denmark, and Danes believe that they have been largely overcome.

That such rules[27] *are* xenophobic is illustrated not just by the fact that they are a superimposition over some extant (but now rendered invisible) prejudices and/or victims of old xenophobia—for instance, such rules would automatically affect and forbid marriage with Asians and Africans more than marriage with Europeans—but also by the fact that, implicitly, they create two classes of human beings. A Dane, for instance, can marry another Dane even if both of them are under the age of 24 years and neither of them passes the 'self-support' requirement. Such rules also allow effective ways out to citizens of First World nations (mostly, but not only, white). This is explicitly laid down in the 'immigration test' rule, but it is even more effective in an implicit manner, for instance, the fact that EU citizens, or even US citizens, can move and stay and work more freely in Denmark, by virtue of mutual visa arrangements and other understandings, than Indian or Nigerian citizens can. So, in effect, two classes of human beings are created—as they were by racism—and to some extent these classes overlap with the old demarcations of racism, except that now this has been made almost invisible.

Finally, the empowerment of high capital, which is basically what these rules buttress and protect, is totally obscured. Any attempt to highlight that such occlusion has xenophobic aspects becomes an exercise in differentialist politics, and is then seen as closer to the racism of old xenophobia, so that at times it is the *victim* who comes across as xenophobic and even racist, as almost all Right-leaning European politicians stress these days. This is not to say that versions of xenophobia do not exist among, say, coloured immigrants; but this remains a matter different from the structure of new xenophobia, which is not faced up to, and which is even privileged as the correct and fair state of political being. Hidden behind all of this, it need hardly be said, lies the unfaced problem of the free circulation of high capital, and its role in sustaining wealth and social standards in rich countries, and the progressively constrained circulation of labour in a system in which, in theory, capital, labour, and goods are 'free' to circulate.

CONCLUSION | EMOTION, REASON, STRUCTURE

Xenophobia is not so much about unreasonable or reasonable fear of strangers as it is about an unequal and unfair enactment and institutionalization of one's power over others. Reasoning and a power structure are central to this, but, as anyone who has read about genocidal frenzies knows, this does not happen in a bloodless manner: emotions are always at the core of both xenophobia and xenophilia. In this conclusion, we will examine—in the light of our discussion until now—the *emotional impact* of xenophobia, its *reasonability*, and finally the *structure of power* that I argue is essential to understanding and coping with it.

The Emotions of Xenophobia

We have seen that xenophobia constructs strangers as a simplification of the cognitive relationship that the self has with the other. This link between the other and the stranger is central to understanding the emotional import of xenophobia. In *Upheavals of Thought*, Martha C. Nussbaum has defined emotions as 'eudaimonistic[1] evaluations' of a self which is 'constituted (in part at least) by its evaluative engagements with areas of the world outside itself'.[2] She has stressed how emotions arise at the point of self–other distinctions in the infant, and how they are evaluative judgements 'essential to the development of practical reason and the sense of self'.[3] There are convincing grounds for defining at least some major emotions as arising from and at the point where the self encounters 'the world outside itself'.[4] Fear is undeniably one of the most basic and essential for the survival of both the individual and the species. If so, it is not surprising that the encounter of the agential consciousness termed a self[5] with the other, understood very broadly as *another* agential consciousness, can tend to be narrated in terms of heightened, even hysterical, emotions. Terror—or extreme fear—is not the only one. These emotions, as narrated in Gothic fiction, for instance, are an index of the encounter with otherness and an attempt, however incomplete, limited, or unclear, by the self to deal with the other.[6] The bodily aspect of the self–other encounter is always foregrounded in the case of strong or basic emotions. Damasio quotes William James to highlight that a strong emotion is inseparable from the feelings of its bodily symptoms: when one is angry, one's body reacts in some obviously physical ways.[7]

Moments of heightened emotion coincide with confrontations between the self and the other, or a recollection or evaluation of such a confrontation, and the capacity for emotion can also be seen as a recognition, however subconscious, of that (a body/life with *another* consciousness) which is shared by the self and the other, that which exceeds the consciousness-language employed by the self to capture, describe, conscribe, or deny the other. Hence, outbursts of emotion do not just express the self's reaction to the other, they also suggest *something*—not reducible to rationality or language or even the self's consciousness-in-itself—that the self shares in its very 'difference' from the other. In a sense this is similar to the 'face' in Levinas that the self has to recognize as the face of the other who cannot be reduced to the self's language. Like the yet-unnamed Heathcliff, when taken in by the Earnshaws in Emily Brontë's *Wuthering Heights*, the face of the other presents another embodied consciousness and intentionality even though what comes out of that face is just 'gibberish' to the self. The reduction of the unknown language of the other to the gibberish (or the totally knowable evil language) of the stranger is an aspect of xenophobia.

Hence, the very act of making the other totally legible to the self is very different from Levinas's claim that the irreducible other is the source of knowledge for the self. For Levinas's claim stresses the fact that the other, while not simply the negative image of the self, is nevertheless not an end that can ever be known completely: 'Alterity's plot is born before knowledge';[8] 'the other is alterity';[9] the Other is the 'origin of all putting into question of the self';[10] and, above all, the alterity of the Other is 'irreducible to a totality'.[11]

The emotion of terror is always a possibility (but *not* the only one) at the border of selfhood and otherness, otherness and selfhood. Faced with the other, the language of the self breaks down. Later on, it may recover, as Dr Frankenstein's does, and categorize the other in purely negative terms of 'strangeness', as Dr Frankenstein goes on to characterize his monster. But at that moment of confrontation—either as unspeakable surprise or sheer terror or any such fracture—the other is registered in its full alterity, its agency is recognized as independent from that of the self and, hence, at least potentially terrifying. The language of difference that we perforce employ to talk of the self and the other accentuates this potential to terrify, as difference can only be situated in relation to the differentiating self, when in actual fact the relationship of the self and the other is not that of the 'same' and the 'different', but that of the 'same' and the 'non-same'.

If this terror cannot and should not be explained away either as sheer negativity or passing deviation/lack, it can also not be reduced to one face of a possibility. But the *option* of terror/ fear is hardwired into the relation of the self with the other, who is limit and menace as well as possibility and concern. To dismiss either of these broad aspects would be to reduce the other, and in the process reduce the self—for, as Levinas illustrates again and again, not only is the other vital to the self, the self can achieve a completeness only in its acceptance of an ethical relation with the irreducible other, a relation that *can be ethical* only in the context of the 'alterity' of the other.[12] Ethics would not be required if the other could be identical to the self.

This understanding has to be central to any negotiation with xenophobia. It can be divided into these two basic elements: (a) fear of the other, and hence, in social and narrowed terms, any stranger, is one of many options; it is not the only one, but neither is it natural or unnatural, correct or incorrect on its own; and (b) it is a necessary option, not just for evolutionary reasons, but also because it acknowledges the non-sameness of the other from the self.

Xenophobia works with these elements, but contorts them by constructing a particular type of stranger as the other to be feared, thus giving a complex element of conscious existence and cognition (the other) just a narrow and misleading social focus (a stranger). Having done so, xenophobia then implies that fear (and hence hatred) is the only or the most natural reaction. This obscures the larger socio-historical context in which the other always has a face that one can recognize and that 'speaks' to the self outside the language of the self. It also obscures the relationship of the self to the other, which is—as philosophers have argued—vital to the identity of the self. Finally, it bestows on this narrowly constructed social other (as the stranger or foreigner) a legibility—either as extreme negativity (which turns the other into an erroneous anti-self) or as passing difference (which turns the other into just a retarded or delayed self-same)—which is by definition not possible in the self's encounter with the other. These factors explain the *emotional power of xenophobia*. The genuine emotional force of the self's encounter with the other is invested in the xenophobe's reaction to the stranger.

But if the emotional impact of xenophobia is both fact and fiction, it is also a mistake to dismiss xenophobia simply as an error of reasoning (with the implication that xenophobes are somewhat dense people) or a throwback to 'tribal' (implicitly 'stone age') tendencies. As indicated before, from some perspectives xenophobia can be considered a reasoned, correct, or even an inevitable response.

The Reasonability of Xenophobia

Obviously, the evolutionary role of fear should not be ignored, but it fails to explain human forms of xenophobia because of their contradictions, changeability, and subtlety: human beings do not fear the other or respond to fear in ways that are confined to those of other animals, including primates. Various human factors, not least what some people call 'reason', combine to make humans fear others in more complex ways, construct their objects of fear with a far greater variety (or control and thought), and also overcome sheer evolutionary fear in very unusual ways. In other words, some human beings are capable of transferring the evolutionary fear of snakes to a 'rope' and then to a 'Jew' in ways that no primate can master, and human beings, at the same time, can distinguish between a snake and a rope with unmatched complexity and nuance. The expanse of human consciousness—sometimes termed 'reason', though there are credible arguments that reason is only one of the ways in which humans think and experience—enables human beings to identify and differentiate in ways far beyond the capacity of other primates (or animals).

But once we bring reason into the picture, it seems inevitable to many of the good-hearted that xenophobia is just an error of thinking. This is misleading. Jens Rydgren notes that while xenophobic 'beliefs are mostly non-rational from an objective perspective, because of their incongruence with reality, under certain conditions they may appear rational from people's subjective point of view'.[13] While drawing positively on other aspects of Rydgren's paper, I avoid discussions of subjective *or* objective rationality. One can argue that such a redefinition of rationality would leave it a largely useless concept: almost everyone is 'subjectively' rational, ranging from a paranoid man gunning down his neighbour, a teenager massacring a class of kindergarten students, the perpetrator of a nationalist or racist genocide to a mentally challenged individual, a common thief, or a compulsive philanderer.

Instead, I *insist* that xenophobia is a *rational* matter, by and large, no matter how emotionally it might be expressed. As Lupia, McCubbins, and Popkin point out in *Elements of Reason*, rationality is the exercise of rational choice and 'a rational choice is one that is based on reasons, irrespective of what these reasons may be'.[14] Hence, xenophobia and xenophilia can both be *rational* choices—though we might have cause to find some reasons less credible or savoury than other reasons. Given the nature of some of these reasons and our deep (emotional) imbrication in them as human beings, we might not be the best people to call them objective *or* subjective. Also, while we can prove, at times, that some reasons *are* better than other reasons in a given context, this does not mean that the action of adopting any of these reasons is not an exercise in rationality.

True, as Rydgren shows, at least some xenophobic beliefs are due to logical errors: they are often underpinned by categorization and inference biases. Rydgren notes that social actors are confronted with complex and ambiguous situations in daily life which they often sort out by employing inductive strategies of inference.[15] Such inferences are heavily determined by a priori knowledge—which can include cultural prejudices, deeply imbibed xenophobic worldviews, etc.—and information from people/sources one trusts or considers authoritative. In this context, one can understand how and why targets of old xenophobia often overlap with those of new xenophobia, and the role that public pronouncements—such as regular denigration of immigrants, Muslims, 'multiculturalism', etc., by politicians of various shades—play in the promotion of a certain rhetoric.[16]

While allowing for such explanations, I have tried to step beyond and ask a tabooed question: what happens if xenophobia is proved to be the *correct* or *best* or *most functional* 'rational' choice, at least in the sense of standard economic rationality,[17] for instance, in an 'over-populated' world with serious food shortages? What if some xenophobic tendencies can be determined by what may be called 'structural rationality'; that is, by the subject's insertion in dominant structures of power that enable him to exist rationally and materially?

In this book I have tried to see how and why xenophobia can attract some as a form of *correct* or *inevitable* reasoning. What if, in some contexts, the hatred of strangers is reasonable, or seems so? What if, for instance, in a country with unemployment, it seems reasonable to discriminate against newcomers and even debar them access to the job market, as often happens (and is often justified by politicians) in rich—or relatively rich—societies?

The *reasonableness* of xenophobia, particularly new xenophobia, cannot always be dismissed by positing a subjective error; it can only be countered by positing a structural error. It is not a *subjective* error for a worker in a capitalist economy to want the highest-possible salary and the least-possible competition. That, actually, is the reason why so many erstwhile Socialist labour unions in the rich ('advanced') welfare states of Europe do not differ much, except in rhetoric, extent or explanation, from Rightist parties in their opposition to immigrant labour. However, as already illustrated, it can be revealed as a 'structural error': as a failure to comprehend the structures of privilege and power which encompass one's existence.[18]

The Power Structures of Xenophobia

Xenophobia is a *phobia* at least to the extent that it does not simply fear a real danger: for instance, arachnophobes are not just afraid of a very poisonous spider that might fall on them; they are afraid of all kinds of spiders, and even things that resemble spiders or remind them of spiders. That there might be a real danger—for instance, if you encounter a stranger in your bedroom—is a justification used by xenophobes; in effect though, it signals the narrowing down of the vital self–other relationship to a perverse understanding of the other as a hostile and dangerous stranger, and the use of real or perceived threats to empower oneself over the stranger or to legitimize and justify one's power over the stranger. Both emotion and reason are employed for this purpose; but this purpose is primarily enabled—executed—by creating and/or sustaining a power structure in which the stranger is mostly at a disadvantage and, at best, 'tolerated'.

I suggested—without entering the matter in detail, as it would have taken us beyond recorded historical evidence—that very early human societies, on the corollary of other animal societies, must have negotiated power physically and, with increasing sophistication, materially (better tools, weapons, seeds, land, etc.). With the development of productivity and trade and, hence, a medium and social relation of value—money—we encounter a drastic change in the structures of power between human beings. The old structures of power did/ do not fully disappear: for instance, you can still, if you can get away with it, knock down a rich man who strays into your neighbourhood and steal his wallet. Moreover, in the case of high trade—based on production and carrying over from one space to space—money was automatically combined with other physical indexes of power: for instance, strength and hardihood in terms of travel or 'carrying over' of trade goods, or physical skill in terms of producing goods (or crops). Hence, physical and material sources of power remained a part of a high trade and even production-based capitalist 'money' economy.

But money contained an abstract logic that was both revolutionary (in the sense of weakening old physical/material structures of power) and repressive (in the sense of imposing its own abstract structure of power on people and the world worked over by them). Duchrow and Hinkelammert put this in terms not tainted by Leftist/Rightist ideological differences when they point out that there is a structural *asymmetry* in the money economy: '[M]oney owners in a money economy are in a privileged position compared to the owners of a commodity. [...] The latter have to struggle for recognition in the market. [... But] nobody can participate in the market [once a money economy is established] without money.'[19]

In other words, in a predominantly money economy, it makes sense to traffic in money, rather than in commodity. Commodities can go in and out of fashion, but money will always be in fashion as mediating between commodities, no matter which commodity sells best. This takes us to the logic of capital which I consider inherent in money, even though, unlike many Marxists and Liberals, I insist on a distinction between money and capital. Marx in his writings, where he did not always distinguish clearly between money and capital, puts this across in various ways too, for instance, when he points out that capital is always by definition more mobile than labour. It takes time to produce goods or learn skills—to 'retrain', as it is put now—but money-capital can be moved in a moment from one business to another, from one factory to another, and, under globalization, increasingly, from one country to another.

With this restructuring of dominant power—as money-capital—we gradually enter what I examined as the centuries of old xenophobia. In different ways, money-power was an abstraction that stayed rooted in some physical and material realities throughout early trade and production-based capitalism. Most of the forms of old xenophobia that we know—and sometimes erroneously associate with *all* kinds of xenophobia today—were ideological constructs of the period. I illustrated this in different ways in the chapter on slavery-racism, nationalism, and Nazism. At their core was the need to find an abstract justification of currently physical/material structures and enactments of power and, simultaneously, to explain abstract elements of human existence and cognition in 'naturalized' historical or biological terms. As such, even in their bid to seek abstractions, they ended up—covertly and overtly—referring to the existence, real or imagined, of physical differences between the self and the stranger-other.

I argued against a simple reduction of xenophobia to a mistake and/or irrationality, pointing out that from a subjective position it is not a mistake, and that it is almost always a reasoned matter. Instead, I tried to show that there are good structural reasons for the kinds of xenophobia that are prevalent in certain phases of history or certain kinds of socio-economic systems. The stranger-to-be-feared/hated is constructed not just out of cognitive, evolutionary, or psychological matter, but out of very historical socio-economic factors. I traced this construction in the shifting shapes of old xenophobia, which, despite their growing abstraction, returned to a disciplining, tagging, consuming, or exiling of the body of difference qua body, a tendency towards push-out forms of violence. This, I argued, was in keeping with the structures of power in capitalism until recently: as labour, trade, money, etc., capitalism abstracted, but could not significantly erase the body as a location of power.

With high capitalism from the 1980s onwards, this changed: capital abstracted itself, at least in large sections of the dominant classes, even from money. This free-play of capital as numbers—no longer chained to money as medium or social relation—has impacted further on the abstraction of xenophobia. I termed this *new xenophobia* in order to distinguish it in theory—though it is often interlinked in practice—from old xenophobia.

The stranger is constructed by new xenophobia not in physical and material terms, but in abstract ones. This abstraction can be scientific (the recuperation of a heavily ideological theory of genetic inheritance), mathematical (the use of models and charts in a non-contextualized or obfuscating manner), or legalistic, as we examined with the help of some recently framed Danish laws. While the body cannot be evaded totally, it is obscured and wrapped in the king's garment of high capital: this makes the bodies of the in-group and even preferred members of the out-group effectively invisible in their *norm*-alization. It is when the bodies of the out-group start becoming visible, or start making themselves visible, that new xenophobia activates its abstract avenues of power/discrimination to control, erase, consume, or exile them. This is *not* done in the physical/material terms of old xenophobia—colour, race, ethnicity, sexuality, etc.—but in abstract terms, as we have seen.

Old xenophobia constructed the stranger in terms of a physicality or a materiality that was different and had to be feared, and obviously this construction applied to strangers who were already, as implied by my concept of border/contact, not 'unknown'. With new xenophobia, the greater abstraction of capital has shifted the zone of border/contact: we are no longer talking of physical or material differences in such circles, but of a difference between the abstract operation of capital as power—an operation that increasingly marginalizes producing and labouring bodies as well as money today—and the materiality and physicality of human existence. The difference then being constructed is based on the fear of the physical and the material when not mediated through abstract capital. It is not surprising that this process—which need not replace old xenophobia in a coherent manner and is not confined just to the 'west'—runs parallel to increasing theoretical exegesis of the 'body'. Part of this exegesis is a reaction to the abstraction, but part of it is an aspect of it. For instance, when one looks at many of the monstrous, tortured bodies of much of the so-called magical realist, and some of postmodernist, literature, what one notices is the disjunction of pain, and aspects of pain, from the exaggerated or tortured body. Pain, which is essential to an embodied existence, is somehow reduced, even erased, in these accounts of grotesque and afflicted bodies, and this is not coincidental, as the bodies of such fiction have already been abstracted. Here, the body itself becomes an abstraction. While it is not the purpose of this study to go into this matter, one can easily see—not just in fictional, but also in theoretical, practical, economic, and other terms—how a certain celebration of the body in contemporary times abstracts the body into the realm of the immaterial and the non-physical, as just an expression of the many possibilities of the power of abstract capital.

Obviously, an element of xenophobia is narcissism: the stranger is hated because one loves one's identity; the other is feared because one has invested too much in selfhood. What the stranger tells us is mostly what we are, or think we are, not what the stranger is. Hence, the stranger we fear is a good index of our own self-conception. The self-conception of high capitalism is that of a revolution against old structures of 'oppressive' power. These are associated with physical and material manifestations, including those of money as medium and social relation. Instead, the high capitalist self sees itself as above such brutality and violence, and to some extent this is not erroneous: the nature of high capitalism enables power to be exercised in the abstract. The instruments of this power are more abstract than such instruments have ever been. Unfortunately, though, the effect of power is never just abstract, as power is always measured by the self's ability to impact on others and the world. The narcissism of the empowered self, embedded in high capitalism, prevents it from seeing this glaring fact.

If old xenophobia contained an element of this contestation of physical/material power through money-capital—which as medium and social relation had to negotiate between bodies and social spaces—new xenophobia posits its own universal and non-violent empowerment against every other kind of embodied power, whether xenophobic or resistant. This is reflected in the kinds of laws that are framed by the most developed of social democratic countries under new xenophobia, as seen in the latter chapters of this book.

The Way Beyond

Is there a way beyond new xenophobia? To answer this, we have to return to my observation that new xenophobia does not have to do with individual matters—emotion or even reason; it has to do with the structures of power.

This, however, does not mean that the human element can be ignored. Taylor states that 'the great challenge of this century, both for politics and for social science, is that of understanding the other'. He adds that it is no longer possible, as it was until recently, that Europeans or Americans can consider their culture and history as the norm towards which all of humanity was headed, 'so that the other could be understood as an earlier stage on the same road that they had trodden. Now we sense the full presumption involved in the idea that we already possess the key to understanding other cultures and times.'[20]

What Taylor says about the recent centuries of European colonization and imperialism also applies, usually in delimited ways, to what was done by many other non-European elites to their own native others. It could have been the upper-caste and class condescension towards low castes and aborigines in India, the marginalization of Ahmediyas and other minority Muslim sects (as well as non-Muslim communities) in Pakistan, the treatment of Kurds in early twentieth-century Turkey, the forced 'assimilation' of ethnic minorities and Tibetans in China—the list is long.[21]

Common to all such acts is what Taylor has noted about Eurocentric 'presumption': the conviction that 'we' already possess the key to understanding different cultures. That this presumption on the part of non-European elites vis-à-vis their own others was less structured, cohesive, pervasive, and determined than the European version, and that it often borrowed from European discourses of modernity, etc., should not blind us to its presence. It is this that Taylor states (perhaps optimistically, but with some evidence in favour of such optimism) is going to be more difficult in the future.

This obviously involves a human element: both in terms of individual human beings and groups, for instance, when we consider cultural prejudices. This way to cope with xenophobia, old and new, has been predominant. There are repeated efforts to 'educate' people. Most of them seem to fail. And they fail because, as I have hammered away repeatedly in this book from different angles, the structural aspects of xenophobia are seldom taken into account. And at the heart of these structural aspects lies the nature of capital as an instrument of dis/empowerment.

Capital is a pervasive and iconoclastic force: it reduces everything else to a subsidiary. Rooted in the fact that there is, as Duchrow and Hinkelammert put it, a structural asymmetry in the money economy, capital pervades all in due course, reduces everything else to disposable means by which to multiply itself. Workers, consumers, goods, products, factories, even money—all these are finally reckoned and justified in terms of capital. In that sense, the notion of cultural capital is a revealingly misleading one because culture qua culture is never capital. It is not as if all or even many forms of culture imbue its possessor with 'capital', as a legion of struggling artists, writers, linguists, dancers, etc., know. It is capital that makes a particular aspect or fetish of culture profitable. That is why you do not possess cultural capital if you speak Bhojpuri or Maithili because mostly 'globalizing' capital does not circulate via Maithili and Bhojpuri or see any profit in investing in those regions. But you possess cultural capital if you speak English or German. Similarly, it is capital that decides what kind of product, factory, employment, education, art, even hard science—and hence what kind of human being involved in such activities—is 'viable'. This has always been the tendency under capitalism, though, as illustrated, it has increased with high capitalism, for now even money is subservient to capital. Capital is no longer limited to US dollars or Euros or Yen or Rupees. It exists, increasingly, independent of such forms of money, using them only to circulate and multiply itself, in ways that are not dissimilar from how it uses workers, consumers, goods, and 'culture' to perpetuate itself. Finally, capital raises itself to the final and only arbiter of power—and with that, use, beauty, purpose, meaning, and life. The people who are successful under high capitalism are those who accept and further this logic; they are the courtiers of capital. The discrepancy, noted earlier, between the theory of capitalism—which stresses the 'free' circulation of labour and capital—and its practice is simply an aspect of this trend.

This hegemonic, monolithic, and, as Marx put it, vampiric tendency of capital creates vast spaces of opportunity for both old and new xenophobia. After all, at a certain level, both capital and xenophobia operate in similar ways, by dividing the world into the One and the Rest. Capital reduces the multiplicity of human existence and the world, while appearing to promote it. On the one hand, it can, theoretically speaking, turn anything to profit; on the other hand, it reduces, even eliminates, the independent value and meaning of everything else. The entire world is valued only in terms of its ability to further capital. Factories, professions, educations, sciences, arts, lifestyles, regions, even countries are reduced to instruments of capital. This tendency, it is obvious enough, favours the sort of functional and reductive thinking which is at the core of xenophobia. The intermittent shouts of surprise that we hear when Liberals notice that xenophobia has not disappeared with the rise of capitalism is misplaced. The two go hand-in-hand: the abstract stranger is partly a shadow of abstract capital. In that sense, too, the kind of xenophobia that might have existed in pre-capitalist societies would have been different from what I call old and new xenophobia, and hence any justification of current forms of xenophobia with reference to 'tribal' and 'evolutionary' factors is incorrect or dishonest. One can even argue that for xenophobia to exist we need the notion of an *abstract* stranger and this notion might have been more difficult to sustain without an abstract instrument of power, like capital. New xenophobia, in particular, helps in-groups systematically deny the corporeal vulnerability of certain kinds of 'labour'—or what used to be 'labour'—to the abstract violence of capital, while legislating for capital-enabled advantages within the in-group and for its elites.

In short, one way we *cannot* guard against xenophobia is by leaving it to the individual to do so, even though the rights of the individual human being are essential to our endeavour. To return to Taylor, the job of 'understanding' the other cannot be left to the self, or it cannot be left to the self unless some structural changes enable it. Xenophobia has to be prevented in its enactment, which can only be done by ensuring a fair and equal chance to all, including strangers, under any structure of power. There is a need, given the nature of power in high capitalism, to define human rights in such a way as to give equal primacy to employment and work-related rights for all in any given political space. Surely, we cannot talk of the right to shelter, health, or food in a world where all of it depends on the possession of capital without insisting on the right to employment or related compensation for all? In order to do so, structural changes have to be made in the way capital circulates, so that at least the human body, whether working or not, takes precedence over abstract capital and even money-capital. These matters will involve major juristic and legislative challenges at the national and international ('global') levels, as well as a restoration of democratic structures which are not permitted to be curbed by narrow nationalist considerations or hijacked by global capital.

Of course, this will also need to be undergirded by a larger philosophical shift in how we see the human self and its relationship to the world. Levinas, among others in recent years, has argued that the dominant Western bias in favour of freedom is faulty; it is responsibility that comes first. According to Levinas, it is when the self is faced by the other that the self even becomes aware of its freedom to choose. In conceptual terms, we can think of the moment when the consciousness of a self encounters another consciousness (the other), which is recognizable as *another* self, but also by definition non-same from the self. The alterity of the other is essential, and this can be cause for fear. But it is in this moment of facing the other that the self becomes aware of its own self—there can be no self-consciousness without an other who evokes it—and, in that very basic sense, is brought into being as a self. The face of the other, as Levinas puts it, confronts the self with its responsibility. What can and what will the self do in the face of this non-same-self which is the other? What will one agential consciousness do when faced with another agential consciousness, which makes it aware that it is not free to act *unilaterally* upon the world?

Xenophobia steps in here as a convenient response: working on the fear which is just one of the reactions of the self to the other, xenophobia suggests an elimination or reduction of the other. As Jock Young notes, '[t]he desire to demonize others is based on [...] ontological uncertainties' on the part of the self in an in-group.[22] This elimination might be, in Bauman's terms, *anthropophagic* ('annihilating the strangers by *devouring* them') or *anthropoemic* ('vomiting the strangers, banishing them from the limits of the orderly world and barring all communications with those inside').[23] It might involve an 'assimilation' that sets out to reduce the other to more of the self-same, or it might be genocide or concentration camp or banishment or ghetto or the imposition of a different set of laws by which to live (or marry). In both sets of cases, the complexity of the self–other relationship is being evaded: *it might be possible to assimilate or kill the stranger, but it is never possible to assimilate or kill the other.* '[A] foreigner is neither the romantic victim of our clannish indolence nor the intruder responsible for all the ills of the polis. [...] The foreigner lives within us: he is the hidden face of our identity.'[24] Hence, the stranger/foreigner, as a simplification of this other who is tied to the self, who is the 'hidden face of our identity', always returns in some form or the other. We have seen how this happens, as in new xenophobia, even when the self defines itself as 'open' and genuinely opposes older forms of xenophobia.

Xenophobia, then, is a danger inherent in the kind of simplification that reduces otherness to strangeness, just as it is inherent in the kind of simplification that reduces the other to more of the self or an anti-self. One can even define xenophobia, old or new, in such terms. *Xenophobia is the attempt to reduce the other to a stranger and/or to reduce the strangeness of the other in a bid to empower oneself on terms denied to the other.*

Once we face up to this often overlooked but core element in xenophobia, we begin to understand our failure, till date, to tackle xenophobia. The usual attempt to curtail xenophobia by preaching love and mutual respect or espousing multiculturalism—in short, educating people, as individuals or groups (whether an in-group or an out-group or both)—is seriously limited because xenophobia is not primarily about people. It is about power.

Xenophobia is essentially the index of an ongoing power struggle, enabled by the nature of capital, which is why its subjects—the men and women—change, but xenophobia, like the proverbial river, seems to 'go on forever'. It can be seriously addressed by ensuring—constitutionally, legally, economically, etc.—that power struggles (which cannot be avoided) are not institutionally biased against any particular group. In a globalizing and high-capitalist world, this would include mechanisms to promote parity between capital and labour, keeping in mind that the former has no colour, gender, sexuality, or race, but the latter does. It is in this sense that we need to systematically hold not just our bankers and capitalists, but also our legislators and politicians responsible.

The current media tendency to (unwittingly) highlight the structural problems that make xenophobia flourish—in the flawed form of a discourse of 'welfare tourism' in the UK or 'the threat against the welfare state' in France or Denmark—is a beacon of hope. Given the very nature of high capitalism, the remedies being suggested by nationalists, old-fashioned leftists and rightists of various hues are all bound to fail. Rich nations can protect their privileges by patrolling their borders only to an extent. Slowly, such patrolling will impinge on their wealth. We are likely to reach a situation not very dissimilar from what the thinking among the affluent classes had to face in the rich colonial nations of the nineteenth century: they had to stop blaming the laziness of the worker, the degeneracy of the poor, etc., and start creating the *structure* of a fairer society within their nations. This could only be done by facing up to and remedying some structural flaws within the nation, as shaped by classical capitalism in the nineteenth and early twentieth centuries. It seems inevitable to me that today some international structural flaws, as shaped by high capitalism, will have to be remedied 'globally' through concerted public action and legislation: the solution to xenophobia—not its eradication perhaps, but its drastic curtailment—is tied to this long-due endeavour.

8.

NOTES

Introduction

1. Ray Taras, *Europe Old and New: Transnationalism, Belonging, Xenophobia* (Lanham and New York: Rowman & Littlefield, 2009), p. 97.
2. Antonio Damasio, *Descartes' Error: Emotion, Reason and the Human Brain* (London: Vintage, 2006), pp. 161–2.
3. Michel Foucault, 'The Subject and Power', in Hubert L. Dreyfus and Paul Rabinow (eds), *Michel Foucault: Beyond Structuralism and Hermeneutics*, 2nd edition (Chicago: University of Chicago Press, 1982).
4. Emmanuel Levinas, *Difficult Freedom: Essay on Judaism* (Baltimore: The Johns Hopkins University Press, 1990), p. 6.
5. See, in particular, the work of the Nobel Prize–winning economist, Paul Krugman.

Chapter 1

1. Chinua Achebe, *Things Fall Apart* (Oxford: Heinemann, 1986), pp. 100–1.
2. Martha C. Nussbaum, *The New Religious Intolerance: Overcoming the Politics of Fear in an Anxious Age* (Cambridge and London: The Belknap Press of Harvard University Press, 2012), p. 25.
3. Nussbaum, *The New Religious Intolerance*, p. 20.

4. Nussbaum, *The New Religious Intolerance*, p. 57.

5. Taras, *Europe Old and New*, pp. 119–23.

6. Jens Rydgren, 'The Logic of Xenophobia', *Rationality and Society*, vol. 16, no. 2 (2004), p. 123, available at http://rss.sagepub.com/content/16/2/123, accessed on 10 June 2012.

7. Quoted from Kenan Malik, *The Meaning of Race: Race, History and Culture in Western Society* (Houndmills and London: Macmillan, 1996), p. 261.

8. Damasio, *Descartes' Error*, pp. 131–2.

9. Damasio, *Descartes' Error*, p. 124.

10. See, for instance, Nick Lane, *Oxygen: The Molecule That Made the World* (Oxford: Oxford University Press, 2002).

11. It is mistaken to maintain that our spontaneous sympathies are confined to those we know, while our concern for those at a distance must be delegated to the rusty mechanism of abstract reason. Plenty of people feel more passionately about some remote phenomenon than they do about the people next door [...]. You may lose more sleep over a remote famine, or even over a centuries-old political defeat, than you do over your brother's bankruptcy.

See Terry Eagleton, *Trouble with Strangers: A Study of Ethics* (Malden and Oxford: Wiley-Blackwell, 2009), p. 317.

12. Nussbaum, *The New Religious Intolerance*, p. 29.

13. David McNally, *Monsters of the Market: Zombies, Vampires and Global Capitalism* (Chicago: Haymarket Books, 2012), p. 60.

14. McNally, *Monsters of the Market*, p. 60.

15. Israel J. Yuval, 'Jews and Christians in the Middle Ages: Shared Myths, Common Language', in Robert S. Wistrich (ed.), *Demonizing the Other: Antisemitism, Racism and Xenophobia* (London and New York: Routledge, 1999), pp. 88–107.

16. For me 'border/contact' is a composite term used to define how cultural and other differentiation is worked out between the self and the other, without collapsing the matter into a simple binarism or a blurred hybridity.

17. Perry Anderson, *Passages from Antiquity to Feudalism* (London: Verso Classics, 1996), pp. 182–4.

18. Bettina Bildhauer and Robert Mills (eds), *The Monstrous Middle Ages* (Toronto: University of Toronto Press, 2003).

19. Franco Moretti, in particular, makes a convincing argument about the falsity of seeing Stoker's Dracula only as an aristocrat. He locates him, convincingly, in the cycle of late nineteenth-century 'monopoly capitalism' instead. See Franco Moretti, *Signs Taken for Wonders: On the Sociology of Literary Forms* (London: Verso, 1983).

20. Jonathan Lyons, *The House of Wisdom: How the Arabs Transformed Western Civilization* (London: Bloomsbury, 2010), pp. 4–5.

21. See, for example, Ranjit Hoskote and Ilija Trojanow, *Confluences: Forgotten Histories from East and West* (New Delhi: Yoda Press, 2012).

22. Lyons, *The House of Wisdom*, p. 5.

23. Lyons, *The House of Wisdom*, p. 5.

24. Mary Douglas, *Purity and Danger* (London and New York: Routledge Classics, 2002).

25. Douglas, *Purity and Danger*, p. 44.

Chapter 2

1. If the logic of capital is inherent *but not inevitable* in monetarization, then, one can begin to understand why so many religions that were born in the early phase of larger mercantile societies and universal states were suspicious of money. Hence, Axial-age religions are basically sceptical of interest rates; this can be seen in incidents such as Jesus driving the moneylenders out of the temple and the Islamic prohibitions on charging, or living off interest from money loaned to others. Charging interest was unanimously rejected within most of these ethical (religious) communities. Moneylending on terms fixed by moneylenders, which is based on the concept of money spawning money, is the necessary abstraction that, over centuries, leads to capital and even capitalism.

2. Gary Younge, 'Slandering the Roma Is Just Racist', *The Guardian Weekly*, London, 22 November 2013, p. 19.

3. John E. Roemer, Woojin Lee, and Karine van der Straeten, *Racism, Xenophobia, and Distribution: Multi-Issue Politics in Advanced Democracies* (New York: Russell Sage Foundation, and Cambridge: Harvard University Press, 2007), p. 4.

4. Zygmunt Bauman, 'The Making and Unmaking of Strangers', in Pnina Werbner and Tariq Modood (eds), *Debating Cultural Hybridity: Multicultural Identities and the Politics of Anti-Racism* (London: Zed Books, 1997), pp. 47–8.

5. Julia Kristeva, *Strangers to Ourselves*, trans. by Leon S. Roudiez (New York: Columbia University Press, 1991), p. 2.

6. Wistrich, *Demonizing the Other*, pp. 1–15.

7. Mathew Carr, *Fortress Europe: Dispatches from a Gated Continent* (London: Hurst, 2012), p. 4.

8. Carr, *Fortress Europe*, p. 4.

9. Stephen Castles and Mark J. Miller, *The Age of Migration: International Population Movements in the Modern World* (Hampshire and London: Macmillan, 1993), p. 51.

10. Carr, *Fortress Europe*, p. 21.

11. As early as the 1960s, however, even left-of-centre governments such as the British Labour Party had begun to impose new visa requirements and entry restrictions that were specifically designed to curtail Third World immigration, and these efforts intensified during the global recession that followed the 1973 oil crisis. By the mid 1980s, the legal avenues for unskilled Third World migration in Europe had been drastically curtailed across the continent.

See Carr, *Fortress Europe*, p. 22.

12. Anthony Giddens, *The Consequences of Modernity* (Cambridge: Polity Press, 1997), p. 57.

13. Samir Amin, *From Capitalism to Civilization: Reconstructing the Socialist Perspective* (New Delhi: Tulika Books, 2010), pp. 97–8.

14. George Liodakis, *Totalitarian Capitalism and Beyond* (Furnham: Ashgate, 2010), p. 40.

15. Wayne Ellwood, *The No-Nonsense Guide to Globalization* (Oxford: New Internationalist, 2009), p. 83.

16. James Gleick, *Faster: The Acceleration of Just about Everything* (London: Abacus, 2012), pp. 72–3.

17. Amin, *From Capitalism to Civilization*, p. 101.

18. Zygmunt Bauman, *Liquid Modernity* (Cambridge: Polity Press, 2003), p. 151.

19. Samir Amin, *Capitalism in the Age of Globalization: The Management of Contemporary Society* (London and New York: Zen Books, 2000), p. 1.

20. Amin, *Capitalism in the Age of Globalization*, p. 1.

21. Amin, *Capitalism in the Age of Globalization*, p. 1.

22. Amin, *Capitalism in the Age of Globalization*, p. 1.

23. Amin, *Capitalism in the Age of Globalization*, p. 2.

24. Amin, *Capitalism in the Age of Globalization*, p. 20.

25. David M. Herszenhorn, 'Xenophobic Chill Descends on Moscow', *International New York Times*, New York, 14 April 2014, p. 1.

26. Globalization has eroded the power of national states, and therefore demands a globalized management of economic, financial and monetary systems. But the inference drawn from recognition of the fact of globalization, when stated in this way, is inadequate. No economy exists without politics and without a state. Therefore, economic globalization logically requires the construction of a world political system able to respond to the challenge, *a power system capable of managing social compromises at the worldwide level, just as national states manage them at their level.* However, sufficient maturity does not exist in the area, not even among the group of dominant capitalist countries.... It is therefore not possible, objectively, to have a universal currency and thus a world central bank. The currency and the bank imply that the political problem has been solved, which is not the case.

    See Amin, *Capitalism in the Age of Globalization*, p. 22.

27. Amin, *Capitalism in the Age of Globalization*, p. 26.

28. P. Sainath, 'In 16 Years, Farm Suicides Cross a Quarter Million', *The Hindu*, 20 October 2011, available at http://www.thehindu.com/opinion/columns/sainath/in-16-years-farm-suicides-cross-a-quarter-million/article2577635.ece, accessed on 4 May 2013.

29. Siddhartha Deb, *The Beautiful and the Damned: A Portrait of the New India* (London and New Delhi: Penguin, 2012), p. 122.

30. For instance, in Andhra Pradesh, the liberalization of agriculture was based on a report commissioned from the American consulting firm McKinsey by the then chief minister, Chandrababu Naidu, who was loved during his tenure by the press and such august bodies as the World Bank. The report, titled 'Andhra Vision 2020',

cited 'structural reforms carried out in Chile under the dictatorship of Augusto Pinochet as a model for Andhra Pradesh'. See Deb, *The Beautiful and the Damned*, p. 132.

31. See, for instance, John Vidal, 'Rich Nations Face Climate Fury', *The Guardian Weekly*, London, 22–8 November 2013, p. 1.

32. See also Paul Krugman, *A Country Is Not a Company* (Boston: Harvard Business Press, 2009), p. 37.

33. 'In 1990, the *International Organisation for Migration* (IOM) ventured an estimate of over 80 million persons, including migrants whether documented or not. Out of this total, 15 millions were refugees and asylum seekers.' Christopher Pierson and Francis G. Castles, *The Welfare State Reader: Second Edition* (Cambridge: Polity, 2006/2010), p. 4. One must note that if calculated against an estimated world population of *c.* 5,300 million in 1990, this would come to less than 2 per cent.

34. Stiglitz's international bestseller, *Globalization and Its Discontents*, is an incisive and honest (from a basically pro-capitalism side) documentation of the crippling effect of IMF, WTO, and 'globalization' policies on the developing nations, but even he refers to this great and critical discrepancy between the mobility of capital and labour in careful parenthesis:

> What is this phenomenon of globalization that has been subject, at the same time, to such vilification and such praise? Fundamentally, it is the closer integration of the countries and peoples of the world which has been brought about by the enormous reduction of costs of transportation and communication, and the breaking down of artificial barriers to the flows of goods, services, capital, knowledge, and (to a lesser extent) people across the borders.

See Joseph Stiglitz, *Globalization and Its Discontents* (New York: W.W. Norton & Company, 2003), p. 9.

35. Amin, *Capitalism in the Age of Globalization*, p. 32, also in different words by Zygmunt Bauman in *Liquid Modernity*, and, from a liberal capitalist perspective, Stiglitz, *Globalization and Its Discontents*.

36. Giddens, *The Consequences of Modernity*, pp. 52–60.

37. Among others, see Stiglitz, *Globalization and Its Discontents*, pp. 30–1.

38. It has been argued that the earliest significant modern formulation of the welfare state was made by Thomas Paine in his seminal work, *Rights of Man*.
39. Asa Briggs, 'The Welfare State in Historical Perspective', in Pierson and Castles, *The Welfare State Reader*, p. 17.

Chapter 3

1. Steven Pinker, *The Better Angels of Our Nature: The Decline of Violence in History and Its Causes* (London and New York: Penguin, 2011), p. 153.
2. Pinker, *The Better Angels of Our Nature*, p. 153.
3. Pinker, *The Better Angels of Our Nature*, p. 157.
4. Romila Thapar, *A History of India*, vol. 1 (London and New Delhi: Penguin, 1965).
5. William Muir, *The Mameluke or Slave Dynasty of Egypt: 1260–1517 A.D.* (Amsterdam: Oriental Press, 1968).
6. Niall McKeown, 'Greek and Roman Slavery', in Gad Heuman and Trevor Burnard (eds), *The Routledge History of Slavery* (London and New York: Routledge, 2011), p. 19.
7. McKeown, 'Greek and Roman Slavery', p. 21.
8. Paul E. Lovejoy, *Transformations in Slavery: A History of Slavery in Africa* (Cambridge: Cambridge University Press, 2000).
9. Gwyn Campbell, 'Slavery in the Indian Ocean World', in Heuman and Burnard, *The Routledge History of Slavery*, p. 54.
10. Campbell, 'Slavery in the Indian Ocean World', p. 55.
11. Viviana A. Zelizer, *The Social Meaning of Money: Pin Money, Paychecks, Poor Relief, and Other Currencies* (Princeton: Princeton University Press, 1997), p. 25.
12. The bourgeoisie cannot exist without constantly revolutionizing the instruments of production, and thereby the relations of production, and with them the whole relations of society. Conservation of the old modes of production in unaltered form, was, on the contrary, the first condition of existence for all earlier industrial classes. Constant revolutionizing of production, uninterrupted disturbance of all social conditions, everlasting uncertainty and agitation distinguish the bourgeois epoch from all earlier

ones. All fixed, fast-frozen relations, with their train of ancient and venerable prejudices and opinions, are swept away, all new-formed ones become antiquated before they can ossify. All that is solid melts into air, all that is holy is profaned, and man is at last compelled to face with sober senses his real conditions of life, and his relations with his kind.

Karl Marx and Frederick Engels, *The Communist Manifesto: A Modern Edition* (London and New York: Verso, 1998), p. 38.

13. Kecia Ali, *Marriage and Slavery in Early Islam* (Cambridge and London: Harvard University Press, 2010), p. 10.

14. Ali, *Marriage and Slavery in Early Islam*, p. 10.

15. Ali, *Marriage and Slavery in Early Islam*, p. 11.

16. 'Marriage in the ancient and late antique world was inseparable from other forms of control over women. It is misleading to think that marriage subjugates an otherwise independent female to a husband. Rather, females (like subordinate males) were already enmeshed in webs of kin control and mutual obligation.' Ali, *Marriage and Slavery in Early Islam*, p. 11.

17. Ali's painstaking research documents how Muslim jurists dealt with both marriage and slavery (among other things) as instruments of social control (hierarchy) and wealth distribution. Muslim rules often permitted a degree of liberties (especially in family and sexual terms) to slaves and legalized their relationships to their masters—for instance, by bestowing legality to children born of concubines (slave girls sexually used by their masters). At the same time, they clearly equated marriage and slavery to the extent that both were seen as economic transactions in which a type of control, power, or domination was given to the husband (in one case) and the master (in the other) in exchange for some sort of (usually) pecuniary consideration (Ali, *Marriage and Slavery in Early Islam*, p. 12). This power was not absolute, but regulated, so to say, by the implicit terms of the transaction. In both cases, the body being exchanged was a 'goods'—it could have only incidental say in the matter, though the exchangers might be carefully regulated by written or unwritten norms in their case.

18. Gail Labovitz, *Marriage and Metaphor: Constructions of Gender in Rabbinic Literature* (Lanham: Lexington Books, 2009).

19. The sheer number of Africans landed [in the Americas] was astonishing. Taking British America as a whole, the tide of black migration began to swamp the trickle of white migration. By the time of American independence, many more Africans than Europeans had settled in British America. Between 1630 and 1780[,] some 2,339,000 blacks had settled there as opposed to 815,000 whites. Of course[,] the actual proportion of black to white population was the reverse of these figures. So destructive were the demands of slavery. [...] In 1780, despite the waves of Africans landed in British America, the black population stood at just over 1,000,000; the white population was more than 2,250,000.

James Walvin, *Questioning Slavery* (London and New York: Routledge, 1996), p. 29.

20. André Pichot, *The Pure Society: From Darwin to Hitler* (London and New York: Verso, 2009), p. 41.

21. Pichot, *The Pure Society*, p. 44.

22. They had paid for both the ship and many of the slaves with a form of money equally dependent on an act of mutual credibility: an ocean-crossing bill of exchange like those which sustained the trans-Atlantic slave trade and made it as much a trade in credit as a trade in commodities. These were promissory notes which the merchants would have agreed to honour, with interest, some six or twelve months later. [...] And though neither party to the insurance contract that was later the basis for the case could, at the time that the contract was signed, have possessed anything more than an imaginary knowledge of the property [slaves] they had agreed to value at 15,700 pounds, they could and did legally bind themselves to credit that knowledge and, by that act of crediting one another's imagination, brought that value into legal existence.

Ian Baucom, *Spectres of the Atlantic: Finance Capital, Slavery, and the Philosophy of History* (Durham and London: Duke University Press, 2007), p. 15.

23. It needs to be noted that the tragedy on the *Zong* was by no means an exceptional one. Similar accounts exist from the period.

24. Baucom, *Spectres of the Atlantic*, p. 95.

25. Wistrich, *Demonizing the Other*, p. 2.

26. Albert Memmi, *Racism* (Minneapolis and London: University of Minnesota Press, 2000), p. 55.

27. Memmi, *Racism*, pp. 170–80.

28. Benedict Anderson, *Imagined Communities: Reflections on the Origin and Spread of Nationalism* (London and New York: Verso, 1983).

29. Why is it that large patches of potentially homogenous 'one-language' peoples did not formulate an often-xenophobic nationalism before the age of early capitalism or, at least, the rise of the bourgeoisie by way of the burghers? The answer cannot be a 'nationally imagined' people on the basis of language; for one has to explain why such a people needed to be imagined in a codified language and formed into a nation in a particular phase of history. In order to understand this 'need', one has to refer to the basic fact, stressed by D.D. Kosambi among others, that trade is crucial to the development of language. (See D.D. Kosambi's *An Introduction to the Study of Indian History* and *The Culture and Civilization of Ancient India*.) My understanding of this and of related aspects of nationalism is given in Tabish Khair, 'Godly Nations', *Radical Philosophy Review: Journal of the Radical Philosophy Association*, vol. 4, nos 1 and 2 (2001), pp. 229–46.

30. Jane Burbank and Frederick Cooper, *Empires in World History: Power and the Politics of Difference* (Princeton and Oxford: Princeton University Press, 2010), p. 12.

31. Pichot, *The Pure Society*, p. xvi.

32. Speech of Reichsführer-SS Heinrich Himmler at Posen, 4 October 1943. Document no. 1919-PS, Nuremberg Trial (www.codoh.com/incon/inconhh.html). Also quoted by Pichot in *The Pure Society*, pp. 80–1.

33. It is sometimes claimed by some of his defenders that 'survival of the fittest' is missing in that form in Darwin. This is misleading: Darwin does talk of the 'fit' adapting better to changes and the notion of the 'survival of the fittest' can be logically adduced from his theory of natural selection, as it inevitably was by many Darwinians and all Social Darwinists.

34. Pichot, *The Pure Society*, p. 44.

35. Pichot, *The Pure Society*, p. 44.

36. Quoted by Pichot in *The Pure Society*, p. 79.

37. As Aimé Césaire's *Discourse on Colonialism* or Sven Lindqvist's *"Exterminate All the Brutes"* record, Nazi genocide against Jews

and others had a longer history behind it: that of colonial genocide in Asia, Australia, Africa, and the Americas. Such genocide was justified by important thinkers of the time, such as Herbert Spencer and Eduard von Hartmann. Moreover, Pichot points out that while eugenics is today associated with figures seen as sympathetic to the Nazi cause, such as Carrel, as late as 1941, when it was common knowledge that the Nazis were gassing the mentally ill and had sterilized the 'Rhineland bastards' (people of 'mixed' parentage) in 1937, figures like the 'humanistic social democrat' Julian Huxley and the communist H.J. Muller were championing eugenics as 'the religion of the future'.

38. 'Physicians and life reformers frequently claimed that exceptional beauty was a sign of racial superiority. Only members of the white race, they argued, could come close to the ideals of beauty of the ancient Greeks.' Michael Hau, *The Cult of Health and Beauty in Germany: A Social History, 1890–1930* (Chicago and London: University of Chicago Press, 2003), p. 82.

39. Eugen Kogon, *The Theory and Practice of Hell: The German Concentration Camps and the System Behind Them* (New York: Farra, Straus and Giroux, 2006 [1950]), p. 22.

40. Adam Smith, *An Inquiry into the Nature and Causes of the Wealth of Nations* (Hampshire: Harriman House Ltd, 2010), p. 20.

41. Kevin Lewis O'Neill and Alexander Laban Hinton, 'Genocide, Truth, Memory and Representation: An Introduction', in Alexander Laban Hinton and Kevin Lewis O'Neill (eds), *Genocide: Truth, Memory, and Representation* (Durham and London: Duke University Press, 2009), p. 1.

42. Nussbaum, *The New Religious Intolerance*, p. 36.

Chapter 4

1. See Michael Stewart (ed.), *The Gypsy 'Menace': Populism and the New Anti-Gypsy Politics* (London: Hurst, 2012).

2. Nussbaum, *The New Religious Intolerance*, pp. 1–20.

3. Nussbaum, *The New Religious Intolerance*, p. 56.

4. Nussbaum, *The New Religious Intolerance*, p. 56.

5. Nussbaum, *The New Religious Intolerance*, p. 29.

6. Peter Morey and Amina Yaqin, *Framing Muslims: Stereotyping and Representation after 9/11* (Cambridge: Harvard University Press, 2011), p.1.

Chapter 5

1. Pinker, *The Better Angels of Our Nature*, p. xxvi.

2. Pinker, *The Better Angels of Our Nature*, p. 42.

3. Pinker, *The Better Angels of Our Nature*, p. xxi.

4. Pinker, *The Better Angels of Our Nature*, pp. xxi, xxii, 3, 6, 7, 15, 17, 19, and 23.

5. Judith Butler, *Precarious Life: The Powers of Mourning and Violence* (London and New York: Verso, 2006), p. 29.

6. Smith, *An Inquiry into the Nature and Causes of the Wealth of Nations*, pp. 251–60.

7. Pinker, *The Better Angels of Our Nature*, p. xxii.

8. The exceptions would be those rare countries where everyone shares a similarly low-income level (but enough to subsist on) and some political, cultural, and linguistic solidarity.

9. Pinker, *The Better Angels of Our Nature*, p. 33.

10. The matter is even more nuanced that space permits me to explore, and might be changing again in recent decades. For instance, Jim Hicks notes that during World War I, when organized warfare reached its traditional peak, approximately 90 per cent of the dead were soldiers and only 10 per cent, civilians. By World War II, with warfare changing shape again, the ratio was closer to 50/50 and, in recent wars in Cambodia and Rwanda, almost 90 per cent of the dead were civilians. See Jim Hicks, *Lessons from Sarajevo: A War Stories Primer* (Amherst and Boston: University of Massachusetts Press, 2013), pp. 53–4.

11. Pinker, *The Better Angels of Our Nature*, p. 35.

12. Charles Taylor, *Dilemma and Connections: Selected Essays* (Cambridge: Harvard University Press, 2011), pp. 208–9.

13. Pinker, *The Better Angels of Our Nature*, p. xxii.

14. Pinker, *The Better Angels of Our Nature*, p. 133.

15. Butler, *Precarious Life*, pp. 12 and 33.

16. Tuchman, quoted in Pinker, *The Better Angels of Our Nature*, p. 75.

17. Interestingly, Shylock, the beleaguered, insulted Jew in this play, resorts to a kind of 'physical' violence—an ounce of flesh—as response to the social, linguistic, and economic violence done to him by the 'good' Christians of the play.

18. Can one really compare the violence required for and sanctioned by one socio-economic order with the violence of another socio-economic order? Pinker, with his faith in numbers, believes one can. His critics could argue that one cannot.

19. Do bear in mind that all kinds of violence—physical, material, and symbolic—exist in all phases, and are unlikely to disappear totally in any future. Pinker would agree with this statement about violence in general.

20. Pinker, *The Better Angels of Our Nature*, p. 107.

21. Pinker, *The Better Angels of Our Nature*, p. 111.

22. Dale Spender, *Man Made Language*, 2nd edition (London and New York: Pandora, 1985), pp. 15–18.

23. See, for documents, speeches, and first-hand accounts from the 'Black Freedom Struggle, 1954–1990', Clayborne Carson, David J. Garrow, Gerald Gill, Vincent Harding, and Darlene Clark Hine (eds), *The Eyes on the Prize: Civil Rights Reader* (New York: Penguin, 1991).

24. Taranand Viyogi, one of the best-known Maithili writers from Bihar, an Indian state of much poverty and a large indigenous population, puts his objection to the construction of dams on rivers in these words:

> I have a huge objection with the theory which believes in bringing development by tying down the river. It has to be considered that a river like Koshi can't just be a 'river'; it is the carrier of a certain culture and life style. If you try to tie it down forcefully, then you should remember that you are also interrupting the life-order in an illegal and undemocratic way.

See 'Incision: Tarachand Viyogi interviewed and translated by Prabhat Jha', *Collage*, Fall edition (Patna: Graffiti, 2012), p. 24.

25. Pinker, *The Better Angels of Our Nature*, p. 133.

26. As Kogon, among others, notes, Nazi concentration-camp guards 'who showed softness, "sentimentality", or human sympathy were either kicked out or [...] stripped of their rank before their assembled fellows'. See Kogon, *The Theory and Practice of Hell*, p. 22.

27. Pinker, *The Better Angels of Our Nature*, pp. 50–1.

28. Amin, *Capitalism in the Age of Globalization*, pp. 3–4.

29. Sven Lindqvist, *"Exterminate All the Brutes": One Man's Odyssey into the Heart of Darkness and the Origins of European Genocide*, translated from the Swedish by Joan Tate (London: Granta, 1996 [1992]), p. 66. For a revealing illustration, see http://blogs.smithsonianmag.com/history/2012/11/the-early-history-of-faking-war-on-film/omdurman/, accessed on 11 March 2013.

30. A late nineteenth-century poem by Hilaire Belloc in *The Modern Traveller*, celebrating the advantages of the first proper machine gun in colonial encounters: 'Whatever happens, we have got/ The Maxim Gun, and they have not.'

31. Pinker, *The Better Angels of Our Nature*, p. 51.

32. Do I even need to point out that, given the changes of technology, etc., as was the case of the man shot or stabbed some decades ago, the community flooded or drought-stricken today is more likely to curtail extreme results of that violence, such as death, and this will often be in direct proportion to the affluence of the community?

33. Quoted from Jeremy Seabrook, *The No-Nonsense Guide to World Poverty* (London: Verso, 2003), pp. 24–5.

34. Pinker, *The Better Angels of Our Nature*, pp. 49–52.

35. Pinker, *The Better Angels of Our Nature*, p. 50.

36. Pinker, *The Better Angels of Our Nature*, p. 48.

Chapter 6

1. Morey and Yaqin, *Framing Muslims*, p. 21.

2. Jasbir K. Puar, *Terrorist Assemblages: Homonationalism in Queer Times* (Durham and London: Duke University Press, 2007), p. xi.

3. Puar, *Terrorist Assemblages*, p. xii.

4. Puar, *Terrorist Assemblages*, p. 17.
5. Puar, *Terrorist Assemblages*, p. 25.
6. Mathew Feldman (ed.), *A Fascist Century: Essays by Roger Griffin* (Houndmills and New York: Palgrave, 2008), pp. 181–202.
7. Arun Kundnani, 'Twenty-First-Century Crusaders', in Ziauddin Sardar and Robin Yassin-Kassab (eds), *Critical Muslim 03: Fear and Loathing* (London: Hurst, 2012), p. 47.
8. Kundnani, 'Twenty-First-Century Crusaders', p. 44.
9. Kundnani, 'Twenty-First-Century Crusaders', p. 44.
10. Quoted by Kundnani in 'Twenty-First-Century Crusaders', p. 45, from an official Facebook message posted by EDL on its page on 16 November 2011.
11. Slogans from early EDL protests, quoted by Kundnani in 'Twenty-First-Century Crusaders', pp. 41–2.
12. The anti-Semitism and homophobia of many Islamists are apt illustrations: both were far less pronounced (historians have argued that the terms cannot even be applied mostly) in many, if not all, Muslim societies of the past. But the old xenophobic forms of this new political Islam are also revealed in, say, the 'statements' of Osama bin Laden, with their vacillating reiteration of a hostile, devious 'infidel' other who can only be combated and countered. Despite the political elements of such statements, they are also based on a xenophobic levelling of a diverse people under a single 'repulsive' category: 'Jew', 'American', or 'infidel'. (See Bruce Lawrence [ed.], *Messages to the World: The Statements of Osama bin Laden* [London and New York: Verso, 2005].) Incidentally, despite the 'universalist' aspirations of the original message of Islam to which Islamists want to 'return', the depiction and narration of this hostile 'infidel' other by many Islamists is full of physical and material tropes that we have also identified in forms of old xenophobia in the so-called 'Western' context: hence, the insistence by Islamists on physically located difference and the visibility of this difference.
13. At times this can become a version of old xenophobia in Islamist circles.
14. Michael Crowley, 'Triumph: Here to Stay', *Time*, 15 August 2011, p. 19.

15. Taylor, *Dilemma and Connections*, p. 137.

16. Arun Kundnani, *The End of Tolerance: Racism in 21st Century Britain* (London: Pluto Press, 2007), p. 131.

17. Walter Laqueur, 'So Much for the New European Century', *Chronicle of Higher Education*, 1 May, in *The Last Days of Europe: Epitaph for an Old Continent* (New York: Thomas Dunne Books, 2007), B7.

18. Refer, for instance, to Castles and Miller's *The Age of Migration*, Chris Bayly's *The Birth of the Modern World*, or M. Dummett's *On Immigration and Refugees*.

19. See, for instance, Young, *Postcolonialism*, Lindqvist, *"Exterminate All the Brutes"*, and Curtin, *The Image of Africa*.

20. William Dalrymple, *White Mughals: Love and Betrayal in Eighteenth-Century India* (London: HarperCollins, 2002).

21. See David Nash, *Secularism, Art and Freedom* (Leicester and New York: Leicester University Press, 1992). Also see Tabish Khair, 'The Truth about Secularism', in Ranjan Ghosh (ed.), *Making Sense of the Secular: Critical Perspectives from Europe to Asia* (New York and London: Routledge, 2013), pp. 101–10.

22. Taken from the official source, https://www.nyidanmark.dk/en-us/coming_to_dk/familyreunification/spouses/the_24_year_rule.htm, accessed on 23 March 2013.

23. Taken from the official source, https://www.nyidanmark.dk/en-us/coming_to_dk/familyreunification/spouses/self-support-requirement.htm, accessed on 23 March 2013.

24. Taken from official source, https://www.nyidanmark.dk/en-us/coming_to_dk/familyreunification/spouses/immigration_test/the-immigration-test.htm, accessed on 23 March 2013.

25. Taken from the official source, https://www.nyidanmark.dk/en-us/coming_to_dk/familyreunification/spouses/attachment-requirement/attachment_requirement.htm, accessed on 23 March 2013.

26. Kogon, *The Theory and Practice of Hell*, p. 20.

27. A recent anthology edited by Baumgartl and Favell documents, almost incidentally, how similar legislation, targeting 'non-nationals', has come into existence from the 1980s onwards in France, Austria, and Great Britain, among other countries.

See Bernd Baumgartl and Adrian Favell (eds), *New Xenophobia in Europe* (London and The Hague: Kluwer Law International, 1995).

Conclusion

1. Eudaimonistic means concerned with the person's flourishing. See Martha C. Nussbaum, *Upheavals of Thought: The Intelligence of Emotions* (Cambridge: Cambridge University Press, 2006), p. 31.
2. Nussbaum, *Upheavals of Thought*, p. 300.
3. Nussbaum, *Upheavals of Thought*, pp. 190, 191, 200, and 207.
4. Similar points have been made earlier, though not as fully pursued or elucidated as in Nussbaum. Sartre, for instance, noted that emotion 'signifies ... the totality of the relations of the human-reality to the world'. See J-P Sartre, *Sketch of a Theory of the Emotions*, trans. by P. Mairet (London: Routledge Classics, 2002 [1939]), p. 63.
5. I use 'self' in the sense of an agential consciousness: a consciousness able to act on itself and the world.
6. Tabish Khair, *The Gothic, Postcolonialism and Otherness: Ghosts from Elsewhere* (London: Palgrave, 2010).
7. Damasio, *Descartes' Error*, pp. 129–30.
8. Emmanuel Levinas, *Alterity and Transcendence* (New York: Columbia University Press, 1999), p. 101.
9. Levinas, *Alterity and Transcendence*, p. 103.
10. Levinas, *Alterity and Transcendence*, p. 99.
11. Levinas, *Alterity and Transcendence*, p. 137.
12. Ethics, obviously, would not be called for if the other was identical to the self.
13. Rydgren, 'The Logic of Xenophobia', Abstract, p. 123.
14. Arthur Lupia, Mathew D. McCubbins, and Samuel L. Popkin (eds), *Elements of Reason: Cognition, Choice, and the Bounds of Rationality* (Cambridge: Cambridge University Press, 2000), p. 7.
15. 'When individuals face unfamiliar situations, they have, at least initially, only two alternatives: either to use *a priori* forms valid in other situations or to put trust in information and/or

theoretical propositions received from other people.' Rydgren, 'The Logic of Xenophobia', p. 125.

16. That xenophobia can be 'schooled' against has been shown in a number of studies, such as the report of the 68th European Teachers' Seminar at Donaueschingen, Germany, 19–24 June 1995. See Marie-Claude Muñoz, *The Role of the School in Combating Intolerance and Xenophobia* (Strasbourg: Council of Cultural Co-operation and Council of Europe, 1996).

17. Lupia et al., *Elements of Reason*, pp. 8–9.

18. But the word 'failure' is misleading, as this is a 'failure' that is central to the continued 'well-being' of a certain kind of selfhood, and hence not 'incorrect' per se.

19. Ulrich Duchrow and Franz J. Hinkelammert, *Transcending Greedy Money: Interreligious Solidarity for Just Relations* (New York: Palgrave Macmillan, 2012), p. 14.

20. Taylor, *Dilemma and Connections*, p. 24.

21. See, for instance, Francis B. Nyamnjoh's *Insiders and Outsiders: Citizenship and Xenophobia in Contemporary Southern Africa* (London: Zed Books, in association with Codesria Books, Dakar, 2006). This provides a matching argument of the relationship between labour migration, national identification, and capital in the current context in southern Africa. Other books presenting forms of recent non-European xenophobia, though often in other terms, include: Parvis Ghassem-Fachandi, *Pogrom in Gujarat: Hindu Nationalism and Anti-Muslim Violence in India* (Princeton and Oxford: Princeton University Press, 2012); Susan E. Cook (ed.), *Genocide in Cambodia and Rwanda: New Perspectives* (New Brunswick: Transaction Publishers, 2006); and Rahul Pandita, *Our Moon Had Blood Clots: The Exodus of Kashmiri Pandits* (New Delhi: Vintage/Random, 2013).

22. Jock Young, *The Exclusive Society: Social Exclusion, Crime and Difference in Late Modernity* (London: SAGE, 1999), p. 165.

23. Zygmunt Bauman, in Werbner and Modood, *Debating Cultural Hybridity*, pp. 47–8.

24. Kristeva, *Strangers to Ourselves*, p. 1.

INDEX

ABOUT THE AUTHOR

Tabish Khair is the author of various books, including the poetry collections *Where Parallel Lines Meet* (2000) and *Man of Glass* (2010); the studies *Babu Fictions: Alienation in Indian English Novels* (2001) and *The Gothic, Postcolonialism and Otherness: Ghosts from Elsewhere* (2009); and the novels *The Bus Stopped* (2004), *Filming: A Love Story* (2007), *The Thing About Thugs* (2010), and *How to Fight Islamist Terror from the Missionary Position* (2012). His honours and prizes include the All India Poetry Prize and fellowships at University of Cambridge, Jawaharlal Nehru University, Jamia Milia Islamia, University of Delhi, and Hong Kong Baptist University. His novels have been shortlisted for prestigious prizes in half-a-dozen countries, including the Man Asian Literary Prize and the Encore Award, and translated into several languages. *Other Routes*, an anthology of premodern travel texts by Africans and Asians, co-edited and introduced by Khair (with a foreword by Amitav Ghosh), was published by Signal Books and Indiana University Press in 2005 and 2006, respectively. He has also edited and co-edited other scholarly works.

Khair was born into a genteel multilingual Muslim family in 1966—his father, grandfather, and great-grandfather were all medical doctors, but they had descended from a line of landowning, and (by the mid-nineteenth century) increasingly impoverished but always fiercely independent farmers. Khair received his school and college education (up to master's) in his hometown, the small but historical Gaya in Bihar, India. He started working as a stringer for the Patna edition of the *Times of India* while still in college, and, later, following a conflict with Islamic fundamentalists, which forced him to leave Gaya for a few months, joined the Delhi edition of the *Times of India* as a staff reporter. He published his first book—a poetry collection—as part of a national competition run by Rupa & Co., while still living in Gaya: he was the only winner from a small town in India. Khair left Delhi for Denmark for personal reasons and, after a couple of years of doing 'immigrant jobs' (as a hotel cleaner, house painter, delivery boy, etc.), received a scholarship to finish PhD from University of Copenhagen and later a DPhil from Aarhus University, where he currently teaches.

Khair lives in a village off the town of Aarhus, Denmark.